WE DANCED IN DERBY

Dance Halls, Discos, Clubs and Pubs in the 1960s

Roger Smith

the tap PUBLISHING

First published in the UK by The Tap Publishing
38 Station Road, Derby DE3 9GH.
enquiries@thetap-publishing.com

The right of Roger Smith to be identified as the author
of this work has been asserted by him in accordance with the
Copyright, Designs and Patents Act 1988.

Printed by Print2Demand

ISBN number 978-1-3999-3926-3

Contents

Introduction

Dance has been around for longer than the written language. It's a fundamental and joyous part of human nature and can create happy memories. That's what this book is all about.

In terms of popular culture, the 1960s was perhaps the most exciting, fast-moving and interesting decade of our time. National Service had ended in 1957 and young people had put the austerity of the 50s behind them. What followed was a teenage revolution where they could assert their own identity rather than being clones of their parents. With the economy improving fast and employment on a high, the young had the opportunity to develop solid careers where they could earn good money and enjoy disposable cash, even after paying their parents board money.

This cultural revolution materialised in the world of fashion, popular music, and sexual freedom. At whichever part of the decade it was when teenagers became of age to join the revolution, it became their territory. Whatever music genre had taken control – it became their religion. And whatever 'look' dominated the fashion scene – it became their uniform.

The place where teenagers celebrated their exciting identity and new found freedom was usually on the dance floor. At the beginning of the decade dancing to music would take place in a ballroom, dance hall, community centre or even a church hall. The music would be provided by a dance band, trio or local rhythm group. But the popularity of the 45-rpm vinyl record quickly made it the preferred medium.

A few months before the start of the new decade Mecca opened The Locarno ballroom which became Derby's principal dance venue for most of the decade. Many migrated to this spectacular, modern new venue leaving the old established ballrooms around town to struggle on.

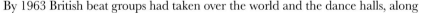

By 1963 British beat groups had taken over the world and the dance halls, along with any hotel or pub with enough space to get in on the action. This made it boom time for local groups and the style of dancing became a bit of a 'free for all'.

In the mid-sixties the burgeoning Mod movement came to the fore and the exclusive band of stylish kids with their love of soul music soon influenced the mass-market. This new culture directly gave birth to Derby's Clouds club and the club scene started to flourish with new venues popping up around the town.

By 1967 the term 'Discotheque' which started in France was quickly adopted by dance venues across the country. Around the same time, the new teenagers joining the scene would have been influenced by Flower Power but it wasn't just them. We saw some die-hard Mods trading their parkas for kaftans, their scooters for Minis, and on the dance floor, swaying dreamily to psychedelic sounds. This soon morphed into a harder and more serious genre which was dubbed Heavy Rock or Prog Rock.

The decade ended with a rise in the popularity of Reggae music which originated in Jamaica.

This book documents a period in the history of popular culture, and the nations love of dance which began well before TV's *Strictly Come Dancing*. Besides doing my best to accurately chronical Derby's most popular dance venues during the 1960s I have shared the memories of the people who frequented them – the dances they did, the music they danced to, and even the clothes they wore.

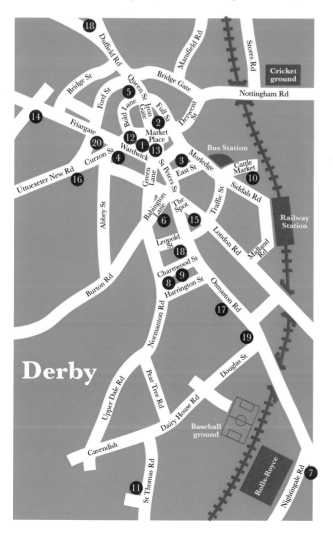

Map Index

1. **Albert Hall (Albert Ballroom)** The Wardwick

2. **Assembly Rooms** Market Place

3. **Central Hall** Exchange Street

4. **Churchill Hall** Curzon Street

5. **King's Hall** Queen Street

6. **Locarno** Babington Lane

7. **Rialto/Stork Club** Nightingale Road

8. **Trocadero** Normanton Road

9. **Balmoral Club** Charnwood Street

10. **Corporation Hotel** Cattle Market

11. **Sherwood Foresters Hotel** St Thomas Road, Normanton

12. **Old Bell Hotel** Sadler Gate

13. **St James's Hotel (Jimmy's)** St James's Street

14. **The Wheel Hotel (Discovery Discotheque)** Friargate

15. **Clouds** London Road

16. **Havana Club** Uttoxeter New Road

17. **Club Italia** Osmaston Road

18. **Polish Club** Osmaston Road & Kedleston Road

19. **Carib Club** Osmaston Road/Douglas Street

20. **Friary Hotel** Friargate

CHAPTER 1: 1960 to 1962
BALLROOM BLITZ

Formal dancing and Rock'n'Roll give way to American Pop

Having established the 'teenage revolution' young people in the late 1950s couldn't wait for the bright and shiny new decade to arrive. They wanted to 'own it' and saw the 1960s as their opportunity to put the past behind them and enjoy their new found freedom and the benefits of high employment.

DANCEFLOOR FILLERS

1. FATS DOMINO.
Be My Guest

2. THE ISLEY BROTHERS.
Shout

3. ELVIS PRESLEY.
It's Now Or Never

4. JOHNNY TILLOTSON.
Poetry In Motion

5. JOHNNY BURNETTE.
You're Sixteen

6. CLIFF RICHARD.
Do You Want To Dance

7. THE DRIFTERS.
Save The Last Dance
For Me

8. CHUBBY CHECKER.
Let's Twist Again

9. CHRIS MONTEZ.
Let's Dance

10. LITTLE EVA.
The Locomotion

Coincidently, on 15th December 1959, just two weeks before the start of the new decade, Mecca opened the Locarno ballroom which became the headquarters of their crusade. At that time the established Derby dance venues included the Assembly Rooms, Trocodero, Albert Ballroom and the Churchill Hall, and although they continued to provide music for dancing with their own resident bands they found it hard to compete with the Locarno.

Mecca employed its own stable of bands at the new Locarno along with the occasional local group. However, although they attempted to re-create the popular dance music of the new decade it was the 45-rpm vinyl record spun by the resident DJ that would become the favourite medium for dancing.

At the start of the 1960s, boys in drape jackets and 'brothel creepers' or smart Italian suits and 'winkle pickers' would dance with bouffanted girls in full skirts. They would Waltz, Quickstep, or Jive to traditional dance music or 50s style Rock'n'Roll. This soon gave way to copious American dance crazes including the Twist, the Locomotion and the Hitch-Hike.

Traditional Jazz (Trad Jazz) became popular in late 50s and early 60s, mainly with the young Beatniks and student population with their floppy jumpers and Ban The Bomb badges. They saw themselves as a small, alternative cult, juxtaposed with the Rock'n'Rollers, and even had their own take on the Jive.

While the traditional dance halls did their best to compete with the Locarno it was clear that their days were numbered. With American Pop Music dominating the charts, and the increasing amount of local rhythm groups making the scene, pubs and hotels were able to take advantage of the social changes that the new decade brought about.

TEN FASHION FAVOURITES

GIRLS

Full skirts with starched petticoats

Gypsy blouses

Elastic belts

Pedal Pushers

Stockings and suspenders

Tweed jackets and skirts

Stiletto heels

Ballet Pumps

Bouffant hair

Straight hair with flick-up ends

BOYS

Drape jackets

Drain Pipe trousers

Lariat tie

Brothel Creeper shoes

Three piece suits

Italian suits

Cut-away Collar shirts

Thin ties

Winkle Pickers shoes

Chisel Toe shoes

Albert Ballroom (Albert Hall)
The Wardwick

One of Derby's oldest dance halls, this historical building was built as an exhibition hall for the Mechanics Institute. It was founded in 1825 to help school leavers as young as 12 to have further education but it didn't become a ballroom until 1895 when it was re-named The Albert Hall as a token of respect for Queen Victoria's late husband. It became one of Derby's most popular venues for dancing well up until the early 60s.

In February 1954 the lease for the ballroom was obtained by local businessman, Sol Lux. It opened a month later after refurbishment and catered for lovers of traditional ballroom dancing with music being provided by some of Derby's top bands of the time including Harold Kite and Syd Arkell.

Albert Ballroom

Towards the end of the 50s, as Rock'n'Roll music started to take over the dancefloors, local groups were engaged to play during the resident dance band's break. These included The Skyliners, The Black Diamonds and The Herald. This format continued into the new decade but little did Mr Lux know that this seismic change in music taste and dancing styles would soon sound the death knell for the venue.

Perhaps an advertisement for the Albert Ballroom in the Derby Evening Telegraph in May 1960 offering 'Select Dancing with Non-Stop dancing to 2 bands' was an indication that the Albert Hall would not be part of the new Swinging 60s.

With the demise of formal dancing, the increased competition from the Locarno, and because the lease had run out, Sol Lux decided to 'throw the towel in' at the end of 1960. A year later part of the building was turned into a shopping arcade called the Haymarket which included Cookes Army Stores and The Scandinavian Coffee Bar. The Mechanics Institute still operated a social club on the upper floor of the same building until the 1980s. At the time of writing the lower floors of this historic building are occupied by the Revolution de Cuba bar.

Central Hall
Exchange Street

Derby Cooperative Society owned the hall which was located on the second floor of its department store in Exchange Street, above the cosmetic and fashion departments. It featured a high, ornate, theatre style ceiling and a professional sprung dance floor. A balcony with raked seating faced the stage. As early as the 1930s it was used as a venue for public dances, private events, concerts and meetings for organisations, associations and clubs.

The Central Hall in 2021

The venue continued to host events well into the early 1960s but, as with the other ballrooms in town, the dances, which tended to target formal dancing, became fewer. However, with the rising popularity of Trad Jazz at the start of the decade The Central Hall presented a 'Jazz Festival' on Friday 9th February 1962 with The Micky Ashman Jazz Band and Chris Blount's Jazz Band.

As the venue was owned by Derby Cooperative Society, and because it could offer a concert style facility for a variety of events, it was able to survive the increased competition from The Locarno Ballroom.

The memories of Don Gwinnett, Allestree.

After doing his National Service playing in the Royal Artillery Band, Don Gwinnett returned to Derby in 1960 and soon became well known around the local dance band scene.

I was stationed at Woolwich Arsenal and played piano in the military band. Back in Derby, it took me a while to get known by other local musicians, so at first, I would go round the various dance halls in town to listen to the local bands. The Albert Ballroom in the Wardwick, run by Sol Lux, was still operating so I was able to listen to the Harold Kyte Band which played for the usual dances of the day - the waltz, foxtrot and quickstep. However, there was also a jive session when the band was able to play jazz numbers such as Stan Kenton's 'Intermission Riff', 'Perdido' and 'Jumpin' At The Woodside'.

The Harold Kyte Band at the Assembly Rooms

The Assembly Rooms
Derby Market Place

Before the opening of the Locarno the old Assembly Rooms in Derby Market Place was perhaps the town's most popular venue for traditional dancing. Couples would Foxtrot, Quick-Step and Waltz to a variety of local dance bands and it was often referred to as 'the marriage bureau'. The dancers mostly consisted of mature youngsters of a marriageable age.

In the early 60s the venue was still attracting decent attendances with the Freddy Sharratt Orchestra playing on Saturday nights and The Syd Arkell Band performing for non-stop dancing on Monday nights.

In February 1963 the roof of the old Assembly Rooms was severely damaged by a fire which weakened the structure of the building. Sadly, the cost of structural repair was too great to be undertaken and the building was condemned, ending its long history as one of the town's main venues for dancing. However, the facade was relatively undamaged by the fire and Derby Borough Council allowed it to be taken down piece-by-piece and rebuilt at the National Tramway Museum in Crich where it still stands at the time of writing.

DISASSEMBLY. The old Assembly Rooms before before being moved to Crich

I was there!

More memories from Don Gwinnett, Allestree.

In the early 1960s the Assembly Rooms was still doing good business with Saturday and Monday night dances. Saturdays featured the Freddy Sharratt Orchestra and on Monday nights it was the Syd Arkell Band. I was involved on several Mondays because, in order to have non-stop dancing, halfway through the evening I would play piano with a couple of members of Syd's band to form a quartet. We would play for about an hour until the rest of the band came back on stage.

RESIDENT BAND The Freddy Sharratt Orchestra on stage at the Assembly Rooms

The original Assembly Rooms was built between 1765 and 1774 and had been one of Derby's principal venues for private and public dance event until its demise.

In December 1962, a few weeks before the tragic fire closed the old Assembly Rooms for good, it presented a Christmas Eve Ball, Boxing Night Ball and a New Years Eve Ball which featured the Freddy Sharratt Orchestra. The local press advertising for these events described the venue as 'Derby's Social Rendezvous', another dig at the increasing popularity of the Locarno. So, while revellers sang a prophetic Auld Lang Syne, the fire would soon bring to an end this historic dance venue. However, even without the fire, it is unlikely that the old Assembly Rooms would have survived as a dance hall.

LAST DANCE
Aftermath
of the fire

Ironically, history would repeat itself in March 2014. Derby's new Assembly Rooms, which was opened in 1977 by the Queen Mother, would suffer the same fate following a roof fire. At the time of writing, the building's future is still undecided.

I was there!

The memories of Don Prime, Quarndon.

I started dancing in the early 50s, Old Thyme Dancing at Rolls-Royce in Nightingale Road and the Community Centre in Boulton Lane, Alvaston. I met my future wife, Pauline, on a blind date at the Trocadero ballroom and dancing became our passion (amongst other things). So, we joined the London School of Dancing which was situated above Hunters furniture store in Babington Lane. This was owned and run by Lawrence Saxleby and Mrs Talbot, and their pupils learnt to dance correctly to the Victor Sylvester rule book. We were regular attendees until the Government decided I would be better spent in uniform (I much preferred the dancing though). After that our social life revolved around dancing and going to Jazz gigs. I have so many memories of the old Assembly Rooms, the Albert Ballroom, the Churchill Hall, and the Kings Hall. Our love of dancing still prevails and celebrating New Year's Eve at The Tower Ballroom, Blackpool, was our annual treat. Oh, such happy times.

Churchill Hall
Curzon Street

During the second half of the 1950s, in the heyday for formal ballroom dancing and Rock'n'Roll, the Churchill Hall presented regular Saturday night dances.

The imposing edifice which still stands in Curzon Street was built for the Temperance Society in 1853 to a design by prolific Derby architect Henry Isaac Stevens. The society's purpose was to encourage abstention from 'the evil drink' and offer self-betterment and a route to salvation. However, it is unclear whether this noble cause continued after it was sold to the Derby Conservative Association in 1946 when it became The Churchill Hall and a dance venue for Derby's young set.

The Grade II listed building in 2021

Dancing took place in the Cinderella Rooms below the main hall, and continued into the early 60s, often featuring the Syd Arkell and Freddy Sharratt bands. A one-off event presented Acker Bilk's Trad-Jazz band before it found chart success with the No.1 hit *Stranger On The Shore*. But these events didn't manage to save it as a dance venue and soon afterwards the building was handed over to the Elim Pentecostal Church which operated there until 2008 after which it was relocated to new premises at Pride Park. In 2019 Curzon Street's imposing Grade II listed building became 'Derby City Church'.

The Churchill Hall pictured in the late 1950s

I was there!

More memories from Don Gwinnett, Allestree.

The Churchill Hall was still very popular for Saturday night dances in the very early 60s when the popular Syd Arkell Band took up the residency. The band usually consisted of four saxes, three rhythm and a trumpet, together with a male and female singer. One amusing story that Syd told me was that he employed an ex-boxer as a bouncer called Darkie Sullivan who came from the West End of Derby. Whenever there was trouble Syd would ask Darkie to go and 'sort it out'. Darkie Sullivan would then put his false teeth in his handkerchief, hand them to Syd and say 'look after these.'

I was there!

The memories of Liz Duffy, Northallerton, North Yorkshire.

In the late 1950s and early 1960s I was in my late teens and early 20s living in Derby. I had a huge circle of friends who were dancing mad, particularly the jive when I wore my full skirts with masses of petticoats and an elastic belt, flat pump shoes and skimpy tops. Those were the days when on Saturday mornings I would get my hair done, huge bouffant style ready for an evening at one of the many dance halls. I frequented most of the dance halls in Derby but my friends and I had our favourites: The Assembly Rooms for special occasions, The Kings Hall for Balls, The Locarno for the big bands and The Corporation Hotel for Jazz. But the best for us was The Cinderella Rooms, below the Churchill Hall. It was a small intimate dance venue, sometimes with a band or a DJ. Everyone got to know each other and the jiving was really electric. It closed at 11.45pm after which many of us went on to a transport cafe on Mansfield Road for breakfast! What happy days – the best years of my life! I am 81 now and a widow living in North Yorkshire, but I dance to all the 60s music every night in my kitchen before bed and re-live those exciting days.

King's Hall
Queen Street

During the winter months, Derby's main public swimming baths in Queen Street were boarded over and used as a dance hall and for other events. On these occasions the venue was renamed The King's Hall and claimed to have the largest dance floor in Derby.

Queen Street Baths

During the early 60s one of its popular annual events was the Hairdressers Competition where salons from around the town would compete for various awards. After the competition the hall would be cleared for dancing to live music.

As with other venues at that time, The Kings Hall's public dance events in the early 60s were also threatened by the opening of the Locarno and they did what they could to stem the tide of dancers migrating to the south side of town. Its advertising in the local press claimed 'Saturday Night is King's Hall Night! The Best Dance in Town'. It kicked off the decade in February 1960 promoting Johnny Clay and his 'Brighter Atmosphere' music. But its programme of events showed little evidence that the promoters were aware of the changing trends in popular music and dance styles. In fact, in the late fifties Jiving was even banned there, and two years into the new decade the King's Hall was still promoting traditional dancing. Derby Corporation eventually managed to catch up with the times and maintain some presence on the Derby dance scene throughout the 60s and well into the 70s. (See later Chapters)

The Locarno 1960 – 1962
Babington Lane

Located at the bottom of Babington Lane, the building was originally built as the Grand Theatre which opened in 1886. The 2,500-seat theatre was designed by Birmingham architect Oliver Essex in an Italian renaissance-style. However, just six weeks after the opening it was badly damaged in a fire which claimed the life of actor John Adams and carpenter James Locksley. It was rumoured to be haunted ever since and when it

The Grand Theatre

was taken over by the May Sum Chinese restaurant in 2007 the owners brought in a medium to rid the building of its ghosts. The Grand Theatre closed in 1950 after being acquired by the owners of the town's Hippodrome theatre. But it stood empty until 1957 when Mecca purchased it with view to turning it into their 'flagship' regional dance hall.

It was totally remodelled with a Canadian pine dance floor, a viewing gallery and a revolving stage. It was hailed as one of the most modern ballrooms in the country.

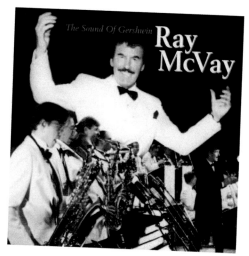

The mayor of Derby, Councillor G A Collier, performed the official opening ceremony of The Locarno Ballroom on 16th December 1959. With a capacity for 1,200 dancers it became the talk of the town and despite its location at the south of the town centre it literally became a 'Mecca' for the young people of Derby with a modernity appropriate for the forthcoming new decade.

I was there!

The memories of Pam Chapman, Stapleford, Nottingham.

The opening of the spectacular new Locarno ballroom created interest from much further afield than Derby and its surrounding area. And for one Nottingham girl it led to a marriage that lasted over 60 years.

I lived in Wilford and, along with my friend June, was a regular at the Palais ballroom in Nottingham. She had heard about this fabulous new ballroom in Derby and that there was lots of 'talent' there. June persuaded me to get the bus over to Derby together to check it out and we weren't disappointed. The Locarno was so luxurious, the resident Ray McVay band were brilliant and the talent wasn't bad either. We were hooked and ended up making the trip to Derby two or three nights a week. One week June couldn't make it and not to be outdone I went on my own. I was watching the band from the balcony and

Pam Chapman (left) and Josie Farmer with Locarno Manager, Alan Ferris

got chatting to Josie Farmer, the girlfriend of the band's pianist, Cliff Hall. She invited me to meet the band during their break and Josie became a dear friend. We would also visit the Barbell Club on Cockpit Hill where she used to keep fit and it was here that I met my husband Eric Chapman who was a member of the club and an amateur photographer. He asked if he could take photos of Josie and I. We met again at the Locarno on a regular basis as part of Josie and Cliff's crowd but one night I was unable to get my usual lift back to Nottingham so Eric offered to drive me home. That's when the romance really blossomed. After dating for a few weeks I had asked Eric what he thought we'd be doing this time next year. His reply was; 'Hopefully we'll be in bed' and I took this as good as a proposal. Eventually Eric did pop the question, on one knee in the foot well of his Ford Anglia.

The Locarno 1960 – 1962
Babington Lane

In line with popular culture of the time the ballroom's interior had a strong Americana theme and included a Ponytail Bar for milk shakes and soft drinks and the New Yorker Bar in a basement area underneath the revolving stage.

Locarno interior

The ladies 'Powder Room' had fitted carpet and dozens of mirrors while the men's 'Stag Room' provided electric shavers and a trouser press.

The ballroom's state-of-the art lighting required a special power unit and featured a huge rotating mirrored glass ball which created a spectacular floor show of hundreds of moving spots in all the colours of the rainbow.

The first men-in-charge were former Leeds Locarno manager, Alan Ferris, and his assistant, Denis Sullivan although, within a few months, Frank Snelling took over as Assistant Manager and proved to be a popular character with Locarno regulars. Music for dancing at the outset was provided by resident bands The Derek Sinclair Orchestra and The Clive Carnazza Trio. The line-up was completed with the employment of local lad, Ross Coe, as resident DJ, or Disc Jockey

as they were called then. Ross would spin the 45s on a button-quilted, twin-deck record console, perhaps the first time twin-decks had been seen in Derby.

In May 1960 Mecca brought in Ray McVay and his orchestra and The Ted Poole Trio as resident bands. McVay enjoyed a golden period of just under two years in Derby after which Mecca rewarded him with a residency in Edinburgh. This didn't please his devotees in Derby who petitioned Mecca to persuade the organisation to re-instate him, but all in vain, and the band left in January 1962 and was replaced for the rest of the year by Jack Massey & his orchestra.

I was there!

The memories of Christine Hardy (nee Blore), Oakwood.

In the late 1950s and early 1960s there were plenty of places for dancing in Derby. But I soon switched allegiance to the modern, new Locarno with its glitz and glamour. For me it was the best venue in Derby for dancing and that marked the start of the best years of my early life - from 16 years old and into my 20s. My first memory is of being at the front of the queue on the opening night in December 1959. I was very excited because it was my first time in a Mecca Ballroom. I remember that one of the resident bands was the Clive Carnazza Trio. The band leader was a very nice guy who gave me a pennant with his photo on, which I have got to this day. However, in my opinion the very best times were when Ray McVay and his orchestra became resident, but I was shattered when, after 2 years at the Locarno, Mecca moved the band to Scotland. I got to know Ray McVay's piano player, Cliff Hall, who married a Derby girl and then became a top session musician before joining The Shadows and spending six years recording and touring the world with Cliff. I went to the Locarno most nights of the week and I loved jiving to upbeat Rock 'n' Roll music. Of course, in line with new chart hits, mainly from the USA, dance styles and crazes quickly changed in the early sixties. This started with the Twist and I also learnt many other novelty dances from this era.

The Locarno 1960 – 1962
Babington Lane

In those early years The Locarno was open seven days a week with lunchtime dance sessions from 12.30pm until 2.00pm on weekdays and an extra hour on Wednesdays to cater for shop girls and boys on half-day closing. Playing the records at those sessions was usually Johnny Whaton, the son of the landlord of the Green Dragon pub on the Spot, Derby.

When I left school in April 1960 I was fortunate enough to get a job on The Derbyshire Advertiser in the Market Place, right in the centre of town. Every lunchtime I would turn towards Mecca - not to the east, but due south on Babington Lane – Mecca's Locarno ballroom. I would position myself on the balcony at the side of the stage and next to one of the massive speaker cabinets. Those Locarno lunchtime sessions, with the anticipation of hearing new sounds and meeting new people, got me through the drudgery of the working day. The Locarno was my church, the disc jockey the preacher and the records he played – my hymns.

The evening line-up included Over 21s Night on Wednesday - popularly dubbed 'Grab a Granny Night' but Saturday was the main attraction of the week, especially after The Ray McVay orchestra became resident.

Teenagers were catered for with an Under 21 Nights every Thursday with the resident DJs spinning the latest hits. These sessions occasionally featured local Rock'n'Roll and Shadows

LOCARNO LADS.
Dave Tice front right.
Fred Bayley front left.
Dave Holman back
right. Pete Wilson
Back left

influenced groups. Under 21 Nights were not licensed to sell alcohol and dancers had to refresh themselves with soft drinks and coffee, but that didn't seem to be a problem for teenagers in those days when Coke and Pepsi were the 'cool' beverages. Saturdays also featured a morning kids club and an afternoon session for teenagers with DJ Ross Coe providing the music.

I was there!

The memories of Dave Tice, Swarkestone.

When the glitzy, new Locarno ballroom opened in December 1959 one young man-about-town made sure that he would make his mark there. Already known for his slick hair style, cutting-edge dress sense and skills on the dance floor, Dave Tice was the ideal ambassador for the new venue. His persona not only reflected the modern style of the spectacular new ballroom but also the optimism amongst the young at the start of the exciting new decade.

I must have been one of the most regular patrons in those early days at the Locarno. We used to go on Wednesdays and Saturdays which were for over 21-year olds. They were terrific nights and beforehand we would congregate at the Cheshire Cheese pub on the Spot. My friends and I would be up for anything. I entered Derby's Best Dressed Man competition because clothes were always important to me, especially my five-button Italian style suit with a white handkerchief poking out of the top pocket. I used to stand in for the resident DJ, Ross Coe, when he took a break and it was with him that I took part in a Mecca publicity stunt by attempting to walk from Derby to London's Lyceum ballroom. Ross completed the walk but I gave up at Kettering and caught the train home. And then, when I turned 21 the Locarno awarded me a golden key. But my main focus was on the dancing, especially jiving - I was famous for having fast feet. In 1960 my partner at the time, Maureen Johnson, and I won Derby's Rock'nRoll Championship despite having cracked a bone in my foot while playing football. More success followed in 1962 when Maureen and I won the Nottingham heat of the Kangol Beret Rock'n'Roll championship and along with our best friends Bob Giovannelli and Christine Burnett, who were winners of the Derby Locarno heat, went off to London to take part in the finals. A London couple won but we had a great time and Mecca paid for us to see Pat Boone at the London Palladium.

THE SILVERWARE

JIVING CHAMPS.
Dave Tice and Maureen Johnson winning the Derby Rock'n'Roll Championship at the Locarno

The Locarno 1960 – 1962
Babington Lane

Friday nights at the Locarno were usually reserved for events hosted by local employers, colleges and associations and the first private dance to be held there was the Master Butchers Annual Ball on Wednesday 6th of January 1960. Derby and District College of Technology Students Union held regular Thrash Nites and on Friday 22nd December presented a Christmas Ball which

Ray McVay and His Orchestra

I was there!

The memories of Jackie Kirk (née Kealey), Littleover.

I have very happy memories of Wednesday nights at the Locarno (our weekly treat after work). I always went with at least five friends, all girls, and in those days nearly all the dancers were single. My friends and I would stand on the balcony looking down at the dance floor at the boys. If one of them saw someone they liked the look of I would go down to the dancefloor to tell him which friend fancied him. At least two of my friends found their husbands at those early Locarno days and have since celebrated their Golden Wedding anniversaries. I also met my lovely husband, Hadge, at the Locarno. For my 21st birthday celebration the Locarno gave me 21 free entry tickets. At the time I was working at Rolls-Royce as a punch card operator and so I gave 20 of my work-mates tickets and, along with their boyfriends, 42 of us went dancing to celebrate my special birthday. On the night I was taken onto on stage where I was presented with a cake and a gold coloured 21st Locarno Key which I still have today. At one Locarno Wednesday evening session a competition was held for girls to come onto the stage to 'cluck like a chicken' and I won! My prize was a voucher for a free chicken from a supermarket on Babington Lane. My mum was super pleased as we could only afford chicken at Christmas back then. When I went to claim my chicken the next day the store manager asked me for a date. He was very good looking and I was single at the time so I said OK. We went to the local swimming baths - bad mistake - me in a rubber swim hat. Unsurprisingly that was our first and last date, but things happen for a reason -I then met Hadge who I went on to marry. We had two beautiful children and I now have 4 wonderful grandchildren. Sadly, Hadge passed away in 1995 but I still have the most wonderful memories including those happy dancing days at the Locarno.

Jackie and Hadge Kirk

featured Cyril Stapleton and his Orchestra, one of the nation's favourite dance bands. Derby Young Conservatives also hosted one-off dance events including Pyjamarama on Friday 21st September 1962 with music from the Clyde Valley Stompers. Perhaps the most popular annual promotion at the Locarno was the Derby Art College Arts Ball which became one of the town's most popular events throughout the 60s.

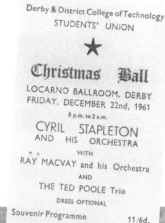

Derby & District College of Technology
STUDENTS' UNION

★

Christmas Ball

LOCARNO BALLROOM, DERBY
FRIDAY, DECEMBER 22nd, 1961
8 p.m. to 2 a.m.

CYRIL STAPLETON
AND HIS ORCHESTRA
WITH
RAY MACVAY and his Orchestra
AND
THE TED POOLE Trio

DRESS OPTIONAL

Souvenir Programme   11/6d.

Locarno Fancy Dress. Left to right Fred Bayley, Dave Tice, Maureen Johnson, Maureen Robinson

More memories from Dave Tice, Swarkestone.

I was there!

After my London adventure competing in the National Rock'n'Roll Dancing finals it was good to get back to the Locarno, my second home, but things weren't all rosy. In January 1962 Mecca decided to move the popular Ray MacVay band to another venue so, along with a couple of friends, we took a petition round saying that we wanted the band reinstated. As a result, the manager, Alan Ferris, banned us from the ballroom until his assistant, Frank Snelling, came to our rescue. He arranged for us to meet with Alan Ferris the next month and he lifted the ban. I was soon back on the dancefloor where my party piece was jiving with two girls at the same time. Girls would often jive together so the way to get to know the one you fancied was to split them up and take them both. The right hand would lead one girl and the left had the other. On one occasion my best friend Bob Giovannelli and I went one step further on the packed dancefloor and split two couples up. He was smaller than me so got on my shoulders and led two tall girls while I took the two smaller girls. I suppose I was a bit of a show-off in those days but everyone seemed to enjoy the performance.

The Locarno 1960 – 1962
Babington Lane

'In the early 60s The Locarno quickly became the place to be, and be seen. Other ballrooms fell into swift decline despite brave challenges from the Trocadero on Normanton Road and the Rialto on Nightingale Road. But by the end of 1962 The Locarno was firmly established as Derby's most popular dance hall and it would continue to thrive throughout the 1960s. (See later Chapters).

I was there!

More memories from Christine Hardy (nee Blore), Oakwood.

I have enjoyed many amazing nights at the Locarno and it was the place to go at Christmas and New Year. Doors would open at midnight on Christmas Day and close at 4.am on Boxing Day, then I would be back again at 8.pm on Boxing Night. I virtually lived at the Locarno and just loved dancing at any time, night or day. When I worked in the offices at Aiton's, on Stores Road, I even went to the Locarno during my lunch break. It was at a Locarno lunch time session that I met my husband, Derek, and we have now been married for over fifty-five years. I also have three sisters-in-law who met their husbands at the same ballroom. The Locarno often hosted the annual balls of local companies and when I worked at Aitons I always entered the 'Miss Aiton' beauty competitions, but always came second or third. What you wore in the dance hall was hugely important. At first, my dancing dresses were flared with an underskirt which had been rinsed in sugared water to keep it sticking out. I had my hair bleached blonde when I was just 15 years old which I had curled

Chris Hardy (nee Blore), right, runner-up in the Miss Aiton competition

A Locarno Beauty Competition

up on top with a French pleat down the back. The benefits of my regular dance 'hobby' was that it was such a great fitness activity. I never tired of dancing and had no qualms about walking home most nights to Leman Street in the Firs Estate area. One thing that sticks out now is how safe Derby was for girls in those days. I feel very sad and nostalgic about the demise of the Locarno, which I called my second home, but at the same time I feel very grateful to have been part of those happy and carefree times.

The memories of Clive Greatorex, Dexter, Michigan, USA.

When the new Locarno opened, I was playing bass guitar in the local group 'Ken Barker and the Jets' and the ballroom periodically held contests to determine the best amateur Rock'n'Roll group in Derby.

Our group did make the coveted first place ranking once, and for a time 'The Jets' were the group to beat and they came to the notice of resident band leader, Ray McVay, who asked my band mate, Ken, if he would like to play guitar with the orchestra on a couple of nights. He soon became a regular addition to the line-up and then I joined him on bass guitar to take over from the traditional double bass on certain numbers. It was a great experience, not to mention that we got into the Locarno free most nights. On leaving school I was quite content with my lot in life - playing in the Jets and the Ray McVay Orchestra, making music and messing around with cars. I was so busy that there was no way I could have a 'real job'. My dad had read that Rolls-Royce was accepting applicants for apprenticeships, so, we had a talk and the conversation ended with a question, 'Why don't you get down to Royce's and see if there's any fear of a start?' That's where my brief but exciting time as a full-time musician ended, but it didn't stop me performing the music I loved in my spare-time, and I still do - 60 years on.

Clive Greatorex (second from right) with his band, Ken Barker and The Jets

The memories of Joe Gunther Willington, Derby.

It was very early in 1960 and everyone was talking about the new Locarno. My friends Steve Winter and Graham Fell decided that we should go and take a look. So, one dark evening we caught the No.88 bus from Sinfin to the Spot in town and turned left into Babington Lane towards the bright neon signs of the Mecca Locarno. I must admit we were feeling a bit apprehensive but excited at the same time. After we had paid and walked through the double doors into the ballroom we couldn't believe our eyes, it was spectacular. For most of the night we stood nervously on the balcony next to the giant speakers, just watching the dancing and the Teds walking round the edge of the dance floor. This was the first of hundreds of visits to the Loc and I soon moved into a flat in town with my friend Barry Clee. We would meet up with other friends on Cockpit Hill and then walk up to the 'Big House' as we called it. Although it was the tail end of the Teddy Boy era we would still be wearing drape jackets, drainpipe trousers and brothel creepers. And very soon it was us that were walking round the edge of the dance hall as if we owned the place. It was our time.

ROLLS-ROYCE WELFARE AMENITIES SOCIETY
MODERN MUSIC GROUP

CHELSEA UNLIMITED

A DANCE WHICH IS DIFFERENT
AT THE MECCA OF DANCING
LOCARNO DERBY
MAY 11th, 1962

ADMISSION 5/-   8 p.m. to 1 a.m.

Licensed Bar   Late Transport
Twist ✴ Rock'n'Roll ✴ Jazz ✴ Dancing

The Jets   Arthur Coyne   Conway
The Heralds   Jazzband   Dance Band
The Electrons   Avon   Gerry Foster
The Black Diamonds   Jazzmen   Swingtet
Jack Massey & his Orchestra   Ted Poole Trio

Trocadero 1960 – 1962
Normanton Road

Around Derby in the 50s and early 60s, the name Sammy Ramsden was synonymous with leisure and entertainment. His Trocadero ballroom was perhaps his most successful enterprise which was opened for dancing in November 1953. Its location on the corner of Normanton Road and Hartington Street started life in 1909 as the Alexandra Roller-Skating Rink and was then converted into a cinema in 1913. Mr Ramsden obtained

Trocodero 1960s

the lease on the building in 1953 when the cinema closed and spent £39,000 on converting it into the Trocadero which he described as "This most super ballroom in England".

Before that, from the mid-1930s, he ran the Plaza Ballroom which was above Sanderson and Holmes, the Rolls-Royce and Bentley car dealership on London Road. But in 1957 he decided to close the Plaza ballroom and told the Derby Evening Telegraph "I find that at my age it is too much to manage the Plaza and the Trocadero". His new ballroom became the town's leading dance venue for the rest of the 50s but it lost its status at the end of the decade, thanks to the Mecca organisation.

FESTIVE FUN. Christmas at the Troc

Despite the threat from the opening of the Locarno in December 1959 Sammy Ramsden wasn't done and he gave the shiny new Mecca ballroom a run for its money. His advertising in the local press was 'fighting talk' with headlines such as "The Ballroom with an Atmosphere". He also hit back with special promotions including free admission for nurses, an offer designed to get Derby's red-blooded young men through the door as well.

The Trocadero continued to be a popular dance venue well into the 60s. Its loyal patrons from the traditional ballroom dancing set continued to frequent the Troc with music provided by resident outfits The Harry Preston Band and The Modernaires Dance Orchestra. Sammy Ramsden also brought top British dance bands to the Trocadero for one-night-stands.

Sammy Ramsden

I was there!

More memories of Don Gwinnett, Allestree.

In the early 60s Mr Sam Ramsden's Trocadero used local bands to provide music for regular weekly dances. However, he also booked top British bands for one-night-stands. Three that I recall are The Squadronaires (led by Ronnie Aldrich on piano), The Johnny Dankworth Orchestra and The Eric Delaney Band. When Eric Delaney came he had just enjoyed a big hit record with his version of 'Oranges and Lemons' and his gimmick was that he played a special arrangement with him playing tympani. I particularly enjoyed the Johnny Dankworth Orchestra and was very impressed by their stage outfits with each section having a different pastel coloured jacket.

I was there!

The memories of Len Southey, ex-Chaddesden, now Allestree.

Len Southey about to leave school to discover Derby's exciting night life

As a young man around town in the early 60s Charles Southey, known to his friends since childhood as Len, recalls his visits to the Locarno and Trocadero ballrooms. Besides the popular music and dance trends of the day, fashion played an important part of the Derby scene as Len explains:

'I left Spondon House school in 1962 and the only venues I can recall where we could dance in those days were the Loc. and the Troc. I wasn't old enough to visit the popular public houses around town, and in any case, pubs tended to avoid dance areas as it often incited alcohol induced fist fights. I don't think there were any knives around then, but perhaps the occasional knuckle-duster. The most popular dances were the Jive and the Twist. And as far as clothing went, I recall buying my first suit from Weaver to Wearer in the Cornmarket - an Italian pin stripe which was made-to-measure with 14-inch bottoms and cost just £7.17.6d. My winkle-picker shoes were from Freeman Hardy & Willis, also in the Cornmarket, at around 25 bob (£1.25p). What I really wanted at that time though was a black shirt and white tie from Beverleys on the Morledge but my dad wouldn't let me buy them so I ended up with a conventional white shirt and black tie until I was a bit older and allowed to choose what I wanted. I can also remember wearing Beetle-Crushers and shirts with the collars turned up which was cool at the time (just like Eric Cantona did at a much later date). To complete my look, flashy waistcoats also found a place in my wardrobe, but after doing the Twist in a waistcoat I would end up sweating cobs. Not a good way to attract the opposite sex.'

Trocadero 1960 – 1962
Normanton Road

On Tuesday 3rd January 1961 the Trocadero started its weekly Olde Tyme Dance Nights featuring the Nottingham String Orchestra. But Sam really needed something more appropriate for what would soon become the Swinging 60s.

The iconic Trocadero building just before demolition

So in February 1961 the Trocadero scored one over on the Locarno by presenting American Rock'n'Roll legend Gene Vincent, famous for his two million selling hit Be-Bop-A-Lula. The dance floor was packed with screaming, mainly female, fans and there wasn't

much room for dancing. He continued with his attempts to attract a younger crowd by engaging local beat groups and Trad Jazz bands that were springing up around town. On one particular Thursday evening in 1961 he presented a 'Festival of Rhythm' with six acts 'Playing for the Twist and Rock'n'Roll' with an admission fee of just 2/6p (12 and a half pence). The line-up comprised The Avon Jazzmen, The Heralds, The Electrons, the Conway Dance Band, Arthur Coyne's Jazzmen and The Temperance (not the one with seven members).

The enterprising Mr Ramsden also made his venue available for private events and promotions, usually on Fridays, for local sporting clubs and charities including The Children's Hospital League of Friends and Venturers FC.

His brave efforts just managed to maintain the Trocadero as a viable business and popular venue until the end of 1963.

TROCADERO

· **Thursday Next:** ·

FESTIVAL OF RHYTHM ·
Six Groups: Avon Jazzmen, The
Heralds, The Electrons, Conway
Dance Band, Arthur Coyne's Jazz-
men, The Temperance—playing for
the Twist and Rock 'n' Roll.
Commencing at 7.45. Adm. 2/6. 43

I was there!

The memories of Lynne Dixon (nee Tomlinson), Ex-Shelton Lock, now Beeston, Nottingham.

Before embarking on a long and varied career in Journalism, Lynne Dixon (nee Tomlinson) grew up in Shelton Lock, Derby, attending Homelands Grammar School for Girls. After doing a full-time course at Derby and District College of Technology, Lynne joined the staff of the Derbyshire Advertiser weekly newspaper, training as a news reporter. Her teenage experiences in Derby included dancing to the music of the day and an unconventional introduction to the fashion scene of the 60s.

I have very fond memories of the Trocadero and the Locarno in Derby, soon after I had left school in the early 60s. While at college at Derby Tech on Normanton Road, my fellow students and I would spend happy lunch hours dancing away at the Locarno on nearby Babington Lane. For some reason, one record that was played a lot at that time and sticks most in my mind was 'Runaway' by Del Shannon. Every time I hear that record today, with its distinctive intro, I think of that happy, carefree time in my life.

One of my first experiences of a night-out on the town without my parents was going to an Arts Ball at the Trocadero with my then boyfriend Clive Cope, an ex-Bemrose Grammar School for Boys pupil. His father owned a butcher's shop, George Cope, at the Blue Peter island shopping centre in Alvaston.

But I digress. The event at The Troc was themed as a 'Pyjamarama' and I wore baby doll pyjamas over black tights. I was a fairly inexperienced 17-year-old and looking back I'm surprised my parents let me go out dressed like that. But then, my dad did come and pick me up in his car at the end of the evening to whisk me off safely home! Clive was resplendent in a striped pyjama jacket over shorts, and sported a pair of heavy black-rimmed spectacles, which I think he probably considered rather Dave Brubeck-ish, as he was into modern jazz at the time. (Gosh, he even let me borrow his Thelonious Monk LP). Only trouble was, Clive's specs had no lenses in them. He didn't actually need glasses; it was all for effect!

The following year the annual Arts Ball was held at the Locarno on Babington Lane and the theme was stone age, again in fancy dress. This time I wore a very short, home-made, Flintstones- style tunic (over tights again, I guess). My mum made it for me from old bits of linen and sacking and she painted her idea of pagan symbols on it. Crazy man crazy! I think the Terry Lightfoot Jazz Band was the star attraction that night.

Another stand-out memory for me is the exact moment I first heard about that exciting new dance craze from America, The Twist. I was in a classroom with a group of other girls at my secretarial course at Derby Tech. It was the last year before the college moved from Normanton Road to the new Kedleston Road site. We were on our lunch break when the most sophisticated girl in the class produced a copy of The Daily Mirror.

PYJAMARAMA. Lynne Dixon and Clive Cope dressed for the occasion

Anyway, the newspaper featured a centre spread all about The Twist which had just arrived from the USA via a catchy pop record by a guy we had never heard of called Chubby Checker. The article showed photos and instructions on how to do the dance moves. One of the instructions I vividly recall was to: 'Make like a Matador'. 'We avidly studied the illustrations and practised the new dance in our classroom. Hilarious! I can also remember the Mashed Potato, the Hully Gully, and the Locomotion, more new dance crazes from America, which all followed a year or so later in 1961 or early 62.

The Rialto
Nightingale Road

The Rialto Ballroom dates back to the late 1930s when Joe Aldred became the owner of the motor garage underneath. Above the showroom was The Clock Dance Hall which provided dance classes and general ballroom dancing. Joe Aldred quickly changed its name to The Rialto and continued to provide a programme of formal dances often featuring the Embassy Band. Whist drives and dance lessons were also on offer.

Derby's Rapids beat group demonstrating The Twist. Back: David Whysall. Front from left: John Benniston, Roger Smith, Ian Lennox, Tony Beardsley

At the start of the 1960s, along with the town's other traditional dance venues, the ballroom's attendances diminished and The Rialto had to swiftly adjust its programme to remain viable and reflect the social changes of the new decade.

Bingo nights were launched in August 1961 and the ballroom added regular beat nights featuring local guitar-based rhythm groups. On Friday 21st December 1962 The Rialto advertised a Pop Twenty Dance featuring The Heralds, The Renegades and The Four Aces.

They rocked to the front

The venue would also cater for privately organised dances and the Rialto continued to function throughout the early 60s and well into the British beat group era. However, further changes of direction would be necessary in the middle of the decade. (See later Chapters).

Winners of the Rialto Rock 'n' Jive championship, Jean Newham and John Hodges

I was there!

Memories from David Vince, Mickleover.

In the early 1960 I learnt to do ballroom dancing at the Victor Sylvester Dance Studio on London Road, Derby and the London School of Dance on Babington Lane. This was after having had previous attempts at the Portland School of Dancing which was on the corner of Portland Street and Pear Tree Street and run by Brenda Webb. I lacked the skill and rhythm at the time and wasn't very good, so I gave up! Much later I was persuaded by two friends to go to Vics, as we called it, and join a beginner's dance class. I also had Latin American lessons at the Carlton School of Dance on London Road next to Sanderson and Holmes garage. I then seemed to "find my feet" and really enjoyed the lessons. A year or so later in September 1961 I entered a ballroom dance contest with my partner, Joyce, at the Derby Locarno. They were very happy times on the Derby dance scene during the 1960s and there was never any crowd trouble.

The Dance Studios

Derby's dance studios were well established by the end of the 50s specialising in classical dances such as the Foxtrot, Quick Step, Waltz and Jive. There were classes for absolute beginners, budding professionals and even children.

By the start of the 60s their popularity was in decline until in early 1962 Chubby Checker changed all that. Along with the rest of the nation, Derby went Twist-crazy and everyone wanted to know how to do it. The dance studios were suddenly in demand again and the Victor Silvester Studio attracted long queues of young people anxious to learn the moves. The studio was situated on the top floor of the Gaumont Cinema on London Road and had a separate entrance to the right of the building which led directly to the studio via two flights of stairs.

Alpha and Portland School of Dancing

Pear Tree Road, Normanton

Carlton Shool of Dance

London Road

Gladys Barber Dancing School

St Peter's Street

London School of Dancing

Abbotts Hill Chambers, Babington Lane

London School of Dancing

The Strand

One of Derby's oldest dance studios was the Alpha which was situated on Pear Tree Road, Normanton. In the early 50s, well before becoming the entrepreneurial owner of the Ritz and Trocadero dance halls, Sammy Ramsden worked there turning the chairs at the end of each session. Perhaps that relatively menial position in the midst of aspiring dancers inspired him to find his own success on the Derby dance scene.

After the Twist craze of the early 60s the dance studios ran out of steam – and members. The new generation of baby-boomer teens took to dancing a pandemic-like distance away from their partners; except when it was 'smooch time' at the end of the evening. Formal dancing went 'underground' and took on cult-like status, kept alive by a select band of enthusiasts. Unfortunately, this signalled the end of the Dance Studio as a viable, commercial venture.

CHAPTER 2: 1963 to 1965
THE BEAT BOOM

British Beat and R&B take over the dance floors

This period probably represents the most dramatic change in popular culture in my time.

The winter of 1962/3 was one of the coldest Britain had ever known. Heavy snow was falling during the New Year celebrations and didn't stop until early March. Temperatures were lower than -20°C in parts of Britain and at times the whole country was paralysed – aeroplanes grounded, roads impassable, schools closed and even snowploughs were unable to make their way through the huge drifts. I remember scraping beautifully patterned ice from the inside of my bedroom window in the mornings (no central heating for us then).

Some people were unable to meet family and friends, not unlike recent Covid times. On top of all that the threat of a nuclear war with Russia hung over our heads and yet, underneath the frozen surface, a cultural incubation was taking place, just waiting to blossom like spring bulbs. Young people sensed change, particularly in popular culture, and thanks to four young lads from Liverpool, pop music would never be the same again.

DANCEFLOOR FILLERS

1. THE BEATLES.
She Loves You

2. SWINGING BLUE JEANS.
Hippy Hippy Shake

3. DAVE CLARK FIVE.
Bits And Pieces

4. THE CRYSTALS.
Da Do Ron Ron

5. MARTHA REEVES AND THE VANDELLAS.
Dancing In The Street

6. THE SUPREMES.
Baby Love

7. THE MIRACLES.
Going To A Go-Go

8. THE WHO.
My Generation

9. GEORGIE FAME.
Yeh Yeh

10. MOODY BLUES.
Go Now

The Beatles

Old institutional ideas around music, fashion, dancing, and even sex, were melting away along with the snow and giving way to an exciting brand-new world. Suddenly, being young was a state to be envied: Mersey Beat, The Mini Car, the pill, Mary Quant, David Bailey, Carnaby Street, the march of the Mods - the young had it all.

The Walls Beat Group contest at The Locarno

Traditional dances like the Waltz, Fox-trot and Jive gave way to more free-style dancing, without touching and even without a partner. Dancing became less formulaic and many just 'did their own thing'. Mini-skirted girls and Beatle-suited boys were doing the Twitch or the Stomp with the blokes often resembling poor impressions of Mick Jagger. The 60s Brit Pop sound, influenced by Merseybeat, was more exciting and upbeat than the hit records from USA teen heartthrobs that had dominated the charts in the early 60s. Dancing became more fun.

Beat groups were springing up everywhere including Derby, and the Shadows-style groups joined the revolution by quickly changing their repertoire and their stage image. The hospitality industry had to respond. The few surviving ballrooms placed their emphasis on beat groups and DJs rather than traditional dance bands. Every pub or hotel, with the room to do it, featured 'live' beat music several times a week.

By April 1963, after the snow had thawed, young people hit the ground running (and dancing) with an infectious spirit that would take over the world. This dramatic development in popular culture mutated quickly into the free-thinking, self expression that exists to this day.

By the end of 1964 the Mod movement, which started with The Modernists in London, quickly spread to towns and cities throughout the land including Derby. Members of this new cult needed to be seen as being 'different' in the way they looked, the music they played and the way they danced. The Mods turned their backs on the British Beat revolution and anything that was seen to be commercial, including the venues they frequented.

This change in modern culture was helped along by the music makers. Most significantly, by the jazz bands which were well equipped to adjust their offerings to serve up the Blues, R&B and Soul music favoured by the new Mods.

For example, the jazz band Graham Bond Quartet became the Graham Bond Organisation with Graham on Hammond organ and alto sax, John McLaughlin on guitar, Jack Bruce on bass and Ginger Baker on drums. Crucially, Bond's quartet effectively created the 'live' circuit and the rest of the decades R&B bands followed. Bond's line-up influenced all organ-based British blues/rock bands that followed in later years such as Colosseum, The Nice, and Cream.

In 1964 the Corporation Hotel was quick to respond to this sea change and successfully challenged the dominance of the Locarno ballroom.

TEN FASHION FAVOURITES

GIRLS

Mini skirts
PVC rain macs
Block coloured A-Line dresses
Pleated skirts
Smocks
Flat shoes
Patterned tights
Vidal Sassoon hair styles
Headbands
Full-length suede and leather coats

BOYS

Beatle jackets
Cuban heel boots
Tab collared shirts with knitted ties
Italian suits with cloth covered buttons
Suede and leather waistcoats
Bell bottom jeans
Cycling Shirts
Hush Puppie shoes
Parallel Levi jeans with red socks
Double-breasted suits

MODS ON THE MARKET PLACE. (from right to left) Diane Hazard, Ray Disney, Lin Francis, Steve Claughton, Joe Gunther, Val Pigeon (partly hidden), Sylvia Reid, Paul Barronofski, Lynne Darby, Liam McGuiness, Frank Hodkinson, Hilary Marple

The Locarno 1963 – 1965
Babington Lane

Early in 1963 the British beat group revolution brought about a change of music policy for traditional ballrooms throughout the land. The mighty Mecca organisation had to respond and, despite still being Derby's leading dance venue, The Locarno in Babington Lane had to compete with the local pubs and clubs

that were presenting local, and even national, groups several nights a week. Although it continued to cater for the older dance fans throughout this period with 'Olde Tyme' and ballroom dancing, these nights were relegated to Tuesday nights. Instead of traditional dance bands topping the bill Mecca placed the emphasis on the new guitar-based beat group line-up which would often include electric organ and a scaled back brass section.

I was there!

The memories of Christine Hardy (nee Bloor), Oakwood.

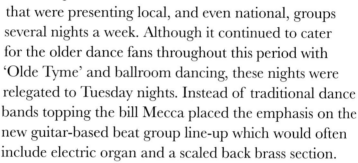

In the early to mid-1960s the Mods (short for Modernists) were shaping and defining fashion. I settled on wearing A-Line dresses with flat shoes.

In those days it was mostly the girls dancing in a circle around their handbags and the boys walking round the dance floor with their mates to work up the courage to cut in. It may sound awful that there were certain individuals you just don't want to dance with, and when you see them hovering on the edges of the Locarno dance floor nearby, waiting to strike when the song ends, you gradually dance over to the other side of the floor. My friends and I would often pull together to avoid pairing off. Larking about one night, we told a group of guys who approached us for a dance, that we were air stewardesses on short layover between flights. In response they said they were all jockeys on a night out. This caused much hilarity for us and we ended up dancing with them. If you turned a boy down when he asked for a dance they would sheepishly go back to their mates (who had been watching their progress) with a bruised ego. I wonder if there are a few oldies around that are still haunted by the memory of being turned down by a girl at a dance.

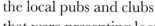

Rolls-Royce (Derby) Apprentices' Association in association with Derbyshire Modern Music Group Incorporating Derbyshire Jazz Groups present

NOVEMBER MADNESS
AT THE MECCA OF DANCING
LOCARNO, DERBY
29th NOVEMBER, 1963
ADMISSION 6/6   8 p.m. to 1 a.m.
Usual Facilities   Late Transport
TWIST - ROCK'n'ROLL - STOMP - TWITCH to the rhythm of the
Heralds   Cyclones   Sapphires   Arthur Coyne Jazzmen
THE FABULOUS BEATMEN
Renegades   Tony Evans Dance Orchestra   Ted Poole Trio

The Locarno 1963 – 1965
Babington Lane

At first Mecca tried to persuade its retained dance bands to re-jig their line-up accordingly. In Derby, for example, the rather dated sounding Tony Evans Dance Band suddenly became Anthony Saint and the Angels. But this didn't always work with ageing dance band musicians trying to perform, gyrate and look like the teenage pop stars that were storming the charts. So, Mecca also employed a few out-of-town beat groups which they moved around its circuit. This, however, didn't go down well with the increasing number of local groups that were enjoying the new beat revolution.

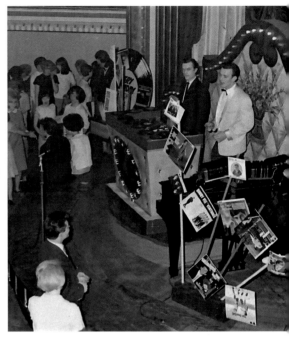

Ian Beniston, spinning the disc with doorman Peter Tomlin

Before this, the Locarno had occasionally booked local groups to perform on Thursday teenage nights, but once they had set-up their own stable of would-be beat groups several local outfits had their bookings cancelled. After letters of complaint to the Derby Evening Telegraph, published in June 1964, the Locarno's Manager, Barry Goodwin, agreed to have local groups back again.

Alvaston group The Vibrons performing on the revolving stage

Once the Locarno had got its act together with regard to presenting dance music that reflected the pop music charts it realised the full business potential. Special one-night events were presented featuring national chart acts including The Dave Clark Five, Freddie and the Dreamers and the Honeycombs.

I was there!

The memories of Mick (Shelly) Shelton, Chaddesden.

After leaving school in June 1962, I started my apprenticeship at Rolls-Royce and soon became a regular at the Locarno's Thursday under 21 nights. These sessions were unlicensed and we had to make do with Coca Cola and coffee. The music and the dancing was influenced by the Mersey beat groups but my closest friends and I weren't really into that music. Our first experience of a club scene in Derby was at 'The Black Cat Club' held at the Kings Hall.

34

But the stand-out performance on the 17th September 1964 was from Herman's Hermits which caused mayhem.

The Manchester group were making its second appearance at the Locarno but this time it coincided with their hit *I'm Into Something Good* reaching No.1 in the charts. That night they had driven to Derby straight after their 'live' appearance on TV's Top Of The Pops. The ballroom's security staff were unable to control the capacity crowd of 1,200 and battled with screaming girls who were trying to get onto the stage to reach lead singer, Peter Noone. Male audience members were recruited to link arms in front of the stage to hold the girls back, some of whom were fainting because of the crush and intense heat. One man had his shirt torn off his back and, after seeing 'bodies everywhere', ballroom manager Don Hall cut short the group's set even before they had performed their chart-topping number.

The memories of Les Wilsoncroft (nee Dix), Derby.

The Locarno was the centre of my universe during that period. I have so many memories but perhaps the most exciting was when I ended up in Urmston, Manchester, sleeping in the living room of Peter Noone's mum's house (Herman of Herman's Hermits). This was after their performance at Derby Locarno on the day their hit 'I'm Into Something Good' went to No.1 in the charts. I was already back stage when the group arrived because I was helping my friend, Carol Simms, get ready as she was a singer with the support group. When Peter Noone arrived in the dressing room, I was star-struck. He looked so cute; I just fell for him. We immediately hit-it-off back stage despite the fact that it was hard to talk above the screaming girls that had packed the dance floor. After the show he just came out with 'Come back to Manchester with me'. My first reaction was 'Er, I'll have to ask my mum'. So, the whole band drove us to Mackworth Estate and waited in the van while I went in to ask my mum'. She didn't like the idea but I told her I was going anyway and off we went. We arrived in the middle of the night and I remember that I slept in the living room which was full of cards and love letters from Herman's Hermits fans and that I met his little Yorkshire Terrier called Androcles. The next morning, I kissed Peter Noone goodbye and caught the train back to Derby to a frosty welcome from my mum. Other memories of the Locarno include me winning the Miss Ziptease competition which was to promote a new fashion brand where their dresses could be transformed into different styles by manipulating various zips within the garments. Then my love of dancing led to me winning the Derby heat of the Brooke Bond PG Tips competition along with my partner for the evening, George Myree, a well-known West Indian guy who was on the scene. I suppose some people thought I was a bit of a 'groupie' and a wild child in those days. Well, I was! But I don't regret a minute of it and I still live by my belief that 'life is for living' (As long as no one gets hurt).

The Locarno 1963 – 1965
Babington Lane

The Locarno continued with its full programme of events designed to provide music and dancing every day and night of the week for all age groups and all tastes. The ballroom's managers during this period were Barry Goodwin in 1963, Don Hall in 1964 and Dave Havell in 1965.

Spinning the platters during that period were resident and part-time DJs including Chris York, Gary Butler, Lawrence Wilson and trainee manager, Ian Benniston.

Ian Beniston in charge of the famous twin-deck record console

Special events included Derby's Best Dressed Man Competitions which I won in 1965 after my girlfriend at the time, Ann Milton, persuaded me to show off my new, made-to-measure, navy double-breasted suit which I had recently purchased from Fred Burns in the Cornmarket.

Beauty competitions were also a popular draw, often as part of the annual dances held for local businesses.

The author, centre, winner of Derby's Best-Dressed 'Moder[n] Young Man' competition in 196[.]

The memories of
Ian Beniston, Wirksworth.

I was there!

I worked at the Locarno from late 1963 until mid-1966. At first, I was just part-time while my day job was working in the offices of Constable Hart the road construction company. I asked for the Locarno job because I was passionate about pop music in general and especially American R&B. I must have impressed because Mecca eventually offered me a full-time job as trainee manager. This involved various roles including my real love spinning the 45s as well as doorman duties and operating the stage lighting for the bands. I was in charge of the lighting on the famous 'Hermania' night and became quite friendly with Herman's Hermits. Later, when they returned to Derby to perform at The King's Hall, I took them across the road for a drink in the Dolphin. Back at the Locarno my main interest was focussed on spinning the vinyl on that iconic padded twin deck console. I was given free license to play what I wanted as long as it was danceable. I also had to include special slots to satisfy all tastes including Tamla Motown and Soul for the Derby's fast-growing Mod movement, a Rock'n'Roll set for the older crowd and, of course, the obligatory 'smooch session' towards then end of the evening. I also worked the Saturday afternoon record sessions and on one occasion when I was acting doorman, I had to deal with a group of lads who were trying to come in but seemed hell-bent on causing trouble. I stepped outside, closing the door behind me to send them on their way but they attacked me. The manager, Dave Havell, had locked the door not realising that I was still outside being beaten to a pulp. I woke up in the Derbyshire Royal Infirmary.

This was the time of the beat groups and Derby's Battle of the Bands became an annual event. Which again brought trouble for the Locarno management and staff.

Local groups each had their own band of, sometimes fiercely loyal, followers and when they came together to support their favourites there was trouble. The 1965 competition followed a public challenge thrown out by one of the area's most popular outfits, The Imps, which saw itself as Derby number-one group. The judging panel included members of the Locarno's resident bands and Roger Groom, licensee of the Corporation Hotel.

The Rapids Big Roll Band on the Locarno stage

In the end the Imps did confirm their claim, with the Cobwebs runners-up, and third place for the band I played in, the Rapids Big Roll Band. Also taking up the challenge were the Carpetbaggers, the Teen Seens, and the Villains.

Battle of the Bands winners, The Imps

A few scuffles ensued between rival supporters but although the Imps were seen as the bad-boys of local groups it was one of our supporters that went a bit too far. One of Derby's notorious characters on the Derby dance scene at that time, Nobby Clarke (real name Michael Hobby), climbed onto the stage during the Imps performance and dragged their lead singer, Terry Buxton, onto the dance floor in an effort to end their performance. It all helped to raise the excitement and tension of the evening and make it a huge success with no real harm done.

I was there!

More memories of Lynne Dixon (nee Tomlinson), Ex-Shelton Lock, now Beeston, Nottingham.

Over a period of two or three years, I regularly went dancing at the Locarno and on one occasion, was dancing round the room when the music stopped and the spotlight fell on me. To my amazement, it was announced that I had been judged Miss Orchid of the evening. And I hadn't even realised that a competition was being held. The next thing I knew I was taken to a back office where they presented me with......yes, that's right, an orchid, and some kind of certificate. I had my photo taken and it still hangs in a frame on the wall of my mum's bungalow to this day!

The Locarno 1963 – 1965
Babington Lane

Right up until the mid-sixties the Locarno was still Derby's most popular dance venue. But towards the end of 1965 there were two sectors of Derby's social scene that were looking for something different.

The teens and early twenties were being influenced by the stylish Mod movement which started in London and the home counties and was quickly finding followers in the provinces.

DERBY AND DISTRICT COLLEGE OF TECHNOLOGY STUDENTS UNION

HEART BEAT
featuring
VIBRONS. THE HERALDS. CYCLONES. STATESMEN. KON-TIKIS. PRESIDANTS.
LOCARNO
21st FEBRUARY 1964
Tickets 5'6. 8pm-1am. Late facilities.
Tickets obtainable from Locarno, Porters Lodges at Normanton and Kedleston Road Colleges and from Committee members. Late Transport to Ring Road, (2 Buses) Allestree, Duffield, Belper, Little Eaton, Kilburn, Heanor, Ilkeston, Chellaston and Melbourne.

At the same time the older sector, perhaps influenced by the new James Bond movies, saw themselves as more sophisticated and wanted somewhere they could dine-out as well as dance and perhaps play a little Roulette, Blackjack or Poker.

Derby group The Heralds on stage at the Locarno

Both these changes in the social habits of the Derby public threatened the dominance of the Mecca Locarno and provided success for both the Corporation Hotel and the new Balmoral club.

I was there!

The memories of Joe Gunther Willington, Derby.

An article I read in the new Sunday Times colour supplement on August 2nd 1964 was like a re-awakening for me. The front cover featured a photo of an 18-year-old Streatham Mod called Denzil and the article, entitled 'Changing Faces', reported on the new Mod culture that was sweeping London and the Home Counties. That was it! I took the photo of Denzil down to John Borrington's barbers shop on Newland Street and asked him to get rid of my quiff and D.A. I bought a Lambretta TV175 scooter and a parka but quickly went for the smarter, Mod look and soon bought many mohair suits and full-length suede and leather coats. At the same time the Corporation became my favourite place for music. In 1965 Derby's first male boutique, Lord Jim, opened at 27 Sadler Gate and although I had no retail experience I applied for the job of 'Manager'. Fortunately, I happened to meet the two Liverpudlian owners in the Bell Hotel's Dilly Bar on the day the boutique opened. I asked them about my application and told them that I was the man for the job. Later that afternoon I hung around in their shop because my friend, Roger Smith, had landed a Saturday job there and I thought he could put a good word in for me. Then, one of the owners just threw the shop keys to me and said 'OK Joe, open up on Monday.'

Corporation Hotel
Cattle Market

Opposite the livestock market, round the corner from the old bus station and the ice factory, stood the Corporation Hotel. It was run by Roger Groom, one of Derby's best-know publicans. It was a favourite watering hole for local farmers on market days and had been in the Groom family since the 1920s.

Photo: Derby Telegraph Archives

In the early 60s it was home to the Abracadabra Jazz Club run by Derby Students Union and when the British beat revolution took hold the Corporation also introduced a weekend programme featuring local groups.

The Abracadabra Jazz Club moved to a different venue in 1964 but Roger Groom decided to continue the Tuesday night Jazz sessions with popular local outfits including The Tommy Owen Band and The Arthur Coyne Jazzmen featuring vocalist Byron T Jackson. National bands also made appearances and top names such as Acker Bilk, Kenny Ball, Terry Lightfoot, Ken Colyear and American saxophonist, John Handy graced the small Corporation stage.

American saxophonist John Handy

Byron T Jackson

Corporation Jazz Club regulars with local band leader Tommy Owen (third from right)

Corporation Hotel
Cattle Market

Around this time the trad jazz boom was beginning to fade and, very quickly, trad jazz clubs went over to a new thing called R&B (Rhythm and Blues). Many of these bands, heavily influenced by British jazzmen Alexis Korner and Cyril Davis, morphed into R&B bands.

Mary and Roger Groom
Photo: Derby Telegraph Archives

RHYTHM & BLUES
Friday—for the first time
THE SYNDI-CATS
Just out—their new record
"Howlin' for My Baby".
Plus V. Rocket's Sound System.
CORPORATION HOTEL
CATTLE MARKET
Next Week: The Art Woods. w/t 37p

Groom was quick to respond to this crossover between jazz bands and beat groups and it turned out to be a master stroke. In summer 1964 he started his Friday Rhythm & Blues nights and went on to present some of the nation's best-known artists and bands.

These included the Graham Bond Organisation, The High Numbers (later to become The Who), Eric Clapton, The Moody Blues, Long John Baldry and The Steam Packet which included Rod Stewart.

I was there!

Monty Sunshine's jazz band at the Corporation Hotel

The memories of Shirley McGuinness (nee Miller) Paignton, Devon. (Formally Mickleover).

A friend of mine asked me to take her to a Corporation Rhythm & Blues night because she had a crush on one of Derby's new Mods, Paul Hopewell. But once she had made contact with her 'prey' she abandoned me. Fortunately, I wasn't on my own for long as one of the Mod crowd took pity on me and came over to talk. He was known as Lee, real name Liam McGuinness, and he asked me for a date on the following Monday, 22nd March 1965. At that time I was a fan of local group, The Rapids Big Roll Band, which included in its line-up a fellow art college student, Doug Smith. I agreed to a date as long as he took me to The Locarno to see the 'The Battle of The Bands' between several local groups. The Imps won and The Rapids came third. That was the start of my love affair with Liam McGuinness and we celebrated our Golden Wedding Anniversary in 2018.

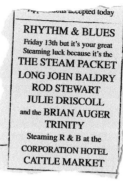

'Rod the Mod' performed a number of times at the Corporation and gained a reputation for always being on the scrounge by asking audience members to buy him a drink or 'crash the ash' (give him a cigarette). I doubt that the star, who was quoted as being worth £215m in the Sunday Times Rich List 2022, has to resort to such measures these days.

THE 'IN' CROWD.
From left,
Helen Sims,
Lynne Darby,
Lyn Reddington,
Lynne Faulkner
Photo: Derby Telegraph
Archives

I was there!

More memories from Helen Faulkner (nee Sims), Borrowash.

The emergence of the Mods movement was perhaps the most exciting time to be a teenager. I was about seventeen at the time and part of a crowd that were considered Derby's 'In-Crowd'.

*It was hard to get Mod clothes in Derby so I used to make a lot of my own clothes on my mother's Singer Sewing Machine. I would buy the fabric from a stall at the open market in The Morledge where there was also Gersh Jacob's stall with some great fashions he'd bring up from London every week. Our favourite night out in those days was The Corporation Hotel where some of the country's top blues and R&B bands played. One of the most memorable nights there was when the Graham Bond Band played which included Long John Baldry and Rod Stewart. After the performance, Rod got chatting to our crowd outside and he told us that Long John Baldry had p****d him off and he didn't want to leave with the rest of the band. He asked if he could hang around with us so we took him up to the Bowling Alley in Collier Street which was the only place still open at that time of night. After that we all went back to my house in Waverley Street, Allenton. It must have been close to midnight but my mum always made people welcome. There must have been about a half a dozen of us including my best friend Lynne Darby, plus 'Rod the Mod'. But my mum didn't know him from Adam - he wasn't famous in those days. I remember that she made us all Coffee (liquid Camp Coffee from a glass bottle). We ended up playing games like Charades until my dad came down stairs with the alarm clock in his hand and shouted at Rod 'Now young man, don't you keep these girls up much longer, I'm on shifts at Royces tomorrow and have to be up at five o'clock!'. I can't remember how Rod got back to his digs in town.*

Helen, right,
with Mod
friend Jenny
Shipman

Long John Baldry
(top, centre) with
the Hoochie
Coochie Men
and a young Rod
Stewart (right)

The Corporation's move into catering for this popular, new genre coincided with the youngsters of Derby being influenced by the new Mod subculture with its penchant for Blues, R&B and Soul music. The Corporation quickly became 'the' place to go for the young dancers of Derby.

Long John Baldry

I was there!

The memories of Mick (Shelly) Shelton, Chaddesden, Derby.

"In early 1963 I had my first 'Mod' experience at the Floral Hall in Great Yarmouth, watching the 'Kinks' performing before the scores of teenagers from London. Back in Derby nothing seemed to have changed until one evening in our favourite coffee bar, the Boccacio, in walked a young man dressed in parallel Levi jeans, a cycling shirt, Hush Puppies and red socks and my whole world changed. His name was Simon Stevenson and he had just moved up from the Home Counties where the 'Mod' movement was taking over. He even had a London accent to complement his image. Soon after that meeting I do believe I became one of Derby's first 'Mods' and the quest to find different clothes began with visits to some unusual shops like the 'Big 6' and 'Nixon's'. There were no alternatives at the time. Very quickly, groups of 'Mod' girls and boys sprung up around town, my set included, Ray Disney, Ron Dawn, Pete Goldsworthy, Clive Raynor, Ian Harvey and Mick Yeomans. We would watch TV's Ready Steady Go on Friday evenings to check out the latest fashion and dance moves. After turning sixteen in August 1963, I was able to ride a scooter and we all adopted the Italian versions of Vespa and Lambrettas, allowing us to visit clubs in other cities such as the Dungeon in Nottingham, the Twisted Wheel in Manchester and the Mojo in Sheffield. In Derby the Locarno and the Corporation R&B Club became our citadels of dance throughout 1964 and into 1965 when casual fashions were overtaken by the 'smart' look and suits became the clothes to be seen in, again we led the way. We just loved being different and would attract some odd looks and sarcastic comments, but we believed that it was better to be noticed than not to be noticed at all."

Gig List

From the diary of Liam McGuinness, Paignton, Devon. (originally Sinfin)
List of performers seen at the Corporation Hotel's Rhythm & Blues Nights

26th June 1964. **Falling Leaves**	6th March 1965. **Rod Stewart**
10th July 1964. **The Pretty Things**	12th March 1965. **Long John Baldry's Hoochie Coochie Men**
14th August 1964. **Long John Baldry**	9th April 1965. **The Sheffields**
21st August 1964. **Falling Leaves**	23rd April 1965. **Alexis Corner**
4th September 1964. **Graham Bond**	30th April 1965. **Graham Bond**
25th September 1964. **Spencer Davis Group**	7th May 1965. **Falling Leaves**
9th October 1964. **Blues & Roots**	2nd July 1965. **John Lee Groundhogs**
13th November 1964. **Moody Blues**	9th July 1965. **Shovelers**
20th November 1964. **Hipster Image**	16th July 1965. **Alex Harvey Band**
27th November 1964. **Tea Time 4**	13th August 1965. **Brian Auger Trinity with Julie Driscoll, Long John Baldry and Rod Stewart**
4th December 1964. **R&B Allstars**	
11th December 1964. **The Birds**	20th August 1965. **Art Woods**
1st January 1965. **The Artwoods**	
8th January 1965. **The Voodoos**	
15th January 1965. **The Sheffields**	
29th January 1965. **Hipster Image**	
19th February 1965. **Alex Harvey Soul Band**	
26th February 1965. **Art Woods**	

The Balmoral Club
Charnwood Street

Derby businessman, Jack Holland, will always be associated with the Balmoral, the club he launched in 1963. During the second World War Jack was posted to the Bahamas as a member of the Air Sea Rescue Unit of the RAF. If he had been a few places forward in the queue to receive his commission he would have ended up in Russia.

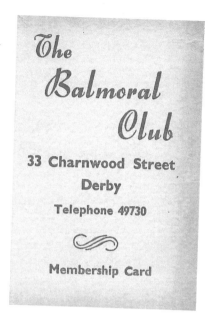

The Balmoral Club

33 Charnwood Street
Derby

Telephone 49730

Membership Card

As you'd expect, Jack blessed his good fortune and became quite attached to the exotic group of tropical islands in a relatively calm part of the world. After the war he returned to Derby and started a taxi firm which worked primarily for local hospitals. He married Winifred in 1947 and had a son, Anthony and daughter, Jill. The couple enjoyed a busy social life in Derby and were regulars on the dancefloors of the Assembly Rooms and the Plaza.

In the mid-50s he moved into property sales and opened Central Estates with offices in Green Lane. Then, in the early 60s, with the Locarno ballroom which was increasingly geared towards young revellers, he recognised a gap in the market.

Jack could see that Derby needed a more sophisticated night spot for the more mature socialite, and one that reflected the famous London night spots. Never short of recognising a business opportunity he quickly made his plan to open the Balmoral Club, the name itself was an inspiration and clearly resonated with the target market. The old United Social Club in Charnwood Street was purchased and totally refurbished.

The Balmoral Club
Charnwood Street

Each room in the Balmoral Club was named after a British castle to reflect the name of the club – the Windsor Bar, the Stirling Room, and the first floor Conway Bar with its dance floor and cabaret stage. Jack Holland had two fellow directors, Geoff Thomas and Jim Gilmore who acted as manager at the time of the opening.

Local jazz singer Mave Pinkney on stage at the Balmoral with pianist Don Gwinnett and Keith Hatton on drums

Over 200 guests attended the 'Grand Opening' of the Balmoral Club on 15th December 1963 which was performed by TV personality Cliff Michelmore. The members-only club became an instant success and was, quite literally, 'the talk of the town'. Besides formal dancing to the resident Ken Barry Trio and other local bands, weekend cabaret nights presented a programme of national names. Winfred's claim to fame is that she 'cut-the-rug' with Lionel Blair. Other big names of the time included Tommy Cooper, Bert Weedon, Chick Murray, Eve Boswell, Yana and even Mandy Rice-Davis who had taken advantage of her fame during the Profumo affair to launch a singing career on the cabaret circuit.

FAMILY NIGHT. The Hollands enjoy a night out at their club

BALMORAL CLUB
(Private Members)
33 CHARNWOOD STREET
Dancing and Dining every evening

TONIGHT

THE FABULOUS
YANA
291c

The Balmoral employed a Head-Chef and experienced catering staff which included two Spanish boys that Jack and Winifred had met on holiday in Spain. Winifred remembers that they were very skilful barmen, juggling with the bottles, glasses and ice cubes – perhaps the first time this kind of performance had been seen in Derby. The menu included the more casual dining favourites of the 60s such as Chicken in a Basket, Steak and Chips and high-end Buffets.

The club was proud of its loyal staff and this was reciprocated despite Jack Holland's very efficient and sometimes strict management style. Winifred remembers that whenever Jack entered the club the caged minor bird which lived on the end of the bar would chirp 'Jacks Back, Jack's Back'.

Jill Holland was a schoolgirl during the Balmoral's hey-day but she was intoxicated by the club's atmosphere, the glamourous members and the exciting cabaret shows. Too young to join in with the fun, she managed to persuade her mother to let her work the cloakroom or even wash glasses behind the scenes so that she could spy on proceedings.

Anthony Holland's budding beat group the Dominators who would practice at the Balmoral. Left to right. Mick Hough, Tony Holland, Roger Wild and Colin Randle with vocalist Cathy Stephenson

At the age of just 14 Anthony Holland was also inspired by the club's music and entertainment and formed his own beat group, The Dominators, which would practice at the club. Although their style of music was perhaps a bit too modern for the club's regulars they did occasionally perform there and backed Bert Weedon during his cabaret act.

A casino was added in a couple of years after the opening and the club went from strength to strength.

I was there!

Memories from Bridie Flood, Alvaston.

I was born in Limerick, Ireland in 1944 but bringing up six children in a country with no social services was very difficult for my parents. In 1953 my father found work at Aiton's in Derby and the whole family moved across the Irish Sea. As an eight-year-old I wasn't that impressed with Derby until I became a teenager. Then I was desperate to go dancing to places like the Trocadero and the Rialto. And when the new Locarno opened, I just had to be there. As Irish Catholics my mother was very strict and I wasn't allowed to go into town in the evenings, but my kind big brother, Eddie, helped me out. He loosened a brick in the outside wall to our house where I was able to hide my lipstick and makeup so that I could get dolled up and go dancing. While I was out, he would hide a wet flannel there so that I could clean myself up on my return. At the age of eighteen I trained as a nurse but the wages were very poor. At that time my big sister Mary was working at the Balmoral club and told me that they were looking for a female croupier for their new casino. Being a bit innocent she had to tell me what a croupier was. So off I went for an interview along with about a dozen other girls who were all dressed up to the nines, and there was I in my nurses uniform. Somehow, I managed to get the job and the man that ran the casino threw my sister a pack of cards and told her to teach me how to shuffle, deal and play Blackjack before I started at the weekend.

Sherwood Rhythm Club
St Thomas Road/Village Street, Normanton

The Sherwood Foresters Hotel on the corner of St Thomas Road and Village Street, Normanton was named after the Sherwood Foresters Regiment which was stationed at the nearby Normanton Barracks. The Sherwood Rhythm Club was formed by Dave Hagues and John Painter in 1963 when the landlord of the Hotel, Dan Beal, agreed to the use of his upstairs function room on Sundays to present local Beat Groups. The Sunday licensing laws of the day required the venue to be 'members only' so they formed the sunday club and set about booking local groups.

Dave Hague was manager of local group The Heralds who later became Six Across and John Painter managed The Statesmen, so both had a good knowledge of the local beat scene. Dave and John would man the door, taking the money and sorting membership applications out. They had help from their girlfriends, Ginny and Margaret, as well as a crate of Double Diamond under the table.

The upstairs room was higher than the average ground floor and getting equipment up there was always a challenge for the bands. When the groups I played bass with, The Rapids Big Roll Band, performed there it took four of us to carry my brother Doug's Lowrey organ up and down the stairs. The club's dancefloor was long and narrow with tables and chairs down each side, a high stage at one end and a bar at the other. Being situated in the busy industrial area of Derby it immediately became a popular venue around the Normanton and Sinfin areas but soon attracted dancers from all over town.

The exterior of the Central Hall in 2021

Black Cat Club - The King's Hall
Queen Street

When it was time for Derby Corporation to board over its Queen Street public swimming baths it became the home of the Black Cat Club which ran on Tuesday evenings. It presented well-known national chart acts including Merseybeat groups, The Mojos (Everything's Alright) and Wayne Fontana and the Mindbenders (The Game of Love).

The venue continued to host private dances at the weekends until the time came to take up the boards and fill the baths with the distinctive smelling chlorinated water which reminds so many 'Baby Boomer' Derbians of their primary school days.

In spring 1963, when the King's Hall was transformed back into the Queen Street public baths, the popular Black Cat Club relocated to the Central Hall in Exchange Street. Sadly, the Queen Street public baths closed in May 2022 and at the time of writing Derby City Council's plans for the use of the Kings Hall had not been published.

Black Cat Club – Central Hall
Exchange Street

When the Black Cat Club relocated to the Central Hall in Exchange Street it continued presenting popular chart acts including Dave Berry and The Cruisers (*Little Things*) but the club's Tuesday night promotions were short lived. Due to the continuing drop in the popularity of formal dance events and private promotions Derby Cooperative Society closed the Central Hall.

It turned this magnificent venue, with its ornate high ceiling and sprung dance floor, over to retail space. It became the Co-op toy department - a rather grand setting for the displays of Sindy dolls, Scalextric and Spirograph.

I was there!

The memories of Bryan Bennion, Normanton.

At the tender age of thirteen I went to my first dance venue at the Black Cat Beat Club which was held at the King's Hall (Queen Street Baths). Three school friends and I had decided to go to see Mersey Beat group, Faron's Flamingos. It was a foggy November night and we arrived early to find the group outside the entrance in a minivan. That little vehicle contained the band members and all their equipment and we helped them in with the gear. They played a lot of Motown songs including The Contours 'Do You Love Me'. I saw lots of bands at the Black Cat Club including Steve Marriott and The Moments before they became The Small Faces, The Mojos, The Big Three, Screaming Lord Sutch and the Savages, Wayne Fontana and the Mindbenders and Johnny Kidd & The Pirates. On the night Screaming Lord Sutch appeared he asked for a volunteer to help them. I was only about 13 or 14 at the time but I put my hand up and climbed on stage where I was helped into a coffin. Then a girl volunteer came on stage pretending to be a vampire and she kissed my neck. I remember Lord Sutch was singing 'I'll Put a Spell on You'.

The Rialto 1963 – 1965
Nightingale Road

In 1963, as Beatle Mania swept the world and British beat groups began to rule the dance floors, the Rialto, along with all other Derby dance venues, had to reconsider their offering. With the help of David Hagues and John Painter, who were enjoying success with their Sherwood Rhythm Club, the Rialto increased its nights featuring local beat groups.

My group, The Rapids, played there on a regular basis and I remember how the ballrooms manager, Les Playdon, always had a cigarette hanging out of the corner of his mouth when he spoke, and he had the uncanny knack of being able to retain about two inches of grey ash on the end of his fag without it dropping on to his suit.

Peter and Gordon

I was there!

The memories of John Colley, Brailsford.

It would be 1963 when I first ventured up the bare concrete stairs and into the shabby delights of the Rialto Ballroom. At the time I was a big jazz fan and a novice saxophonist. I had gone along with a pal, Mick Hough, a budding 15-year-old drummer, when to our surprise we were both invited to join the resident band who were short of their usual members. It must have been sometime in 1965 when I next remember being in the Rialto. They had been presenting the touring R&B bands that were appealing to the new Derby Mod scene. On that particular night I was knocked-out by the dynamic Graham Bond Organisation. Graham had been a modern jazz alto saxophonist of some note but, like several other jazzmen, had turned to Rhythm and Blues and now played a roaring Hammond organ. The rest of the band was Dick Heckstall-Smith (tenor sax), Jack Bruce (vocals and bass) and Ginger Baker (Drums). At the end of the set Baker rose from his drum kit and grabbed a mic to introduce the band, but half way through he collapsed, falling into his scattering kit. He was carried off the stage by the rest of the band, out stone cold. Half an hour later they were back for the second set, Baker back to epic form.

The Rialto also took the bold step of presenting a programme of nationally known names. These included Top 10 chart acts the Applejacks *(Tell Me When)* and Peter and Gordon *(A World Without Love),* the latter being accompanied by drummer Jimmy Nicholl, famous for replacing Ringo Starr on the Beatles tour of Hong Kong and Australia when he was suffering from tonsillitis.

The Rialto had increased success with its popular Tuesday folk nights which saw the occasional top national group performing on its stage. These included the Ian Campbell Folk Group whose version of Bob Dylan's *The Times They Are A-Changin'* reached No. 42 in the UK singles charts.

Jimmy Nicholl

The venue managed to operate with mixed success until the end of this period, but 1966 would sadly see the famous name, Rialto, disappear from Derby for good.

I was there!

More memories from Helen Faulkner (nee Sims), Borrowash.

I lived in Waverley Street, Allenton, round the corner from the Rialto where my brother, Ken, was the bouncer. Despite its out-of-town location it featured some great national and local groups including The Applejacks, The Mojos, Artwoods, and Peter and Gordon who featured Jimmy Nicholl - once a stand-in for Beatle, Ringo Starr, while he was recovering from illness. One night a team from the producers of ITV's 'Ready Steady Go' came in looking for dancers to appear in the audience at one of their shows. They stood around the edge of the dancefloor and if they liked what they saw they would tap on your shoulder. I was dancing with Nobby Clarke (Michael Hobby) at the time and we were selected along with 4 other couples. They bused us down to their studios in London to appear on a show featuring The Swinging Blue Jeans which was presented by Keith Fordyce and Kathy McGowen. It was just about the time that the 'Mod-look' was sweeping the nation. So as soon as I got back to Derby, I copied her distinctive hair style.

Jimmy's (St James Hotel)
St James Street

With its well-established function facilities, including a decent sized dancefloor, one of Derby's oldest hotels took advantage of the British pop group boom by presenting regular Beat Nights. Being located right in the centre of town and close to the terminus for Derby Corporation buses, the St James Hotel, nicknamed Jimmy's, soon became a popular night spot for young revellers to dance the night away. The Club would operate at weekends and Tuesdays presenting 'live' dance music from local and regional groups. One of my most vivid memories of a night out at 'Jimmy's' was on the evening of 22nd November 1963 just before the world-shattering news broke that President J F Kennedy had been assassinated. The news spread quickly around the dancefloor, but astonishingly, I don't remember it putting a damper on the evening. But I suppose that's not that surprising with most young people of the time being totally caught up on the euphoria of the swinging 60s.

Paul Blackmore strutting his stuff on the dancefloor at Jimmy's

Old Bell Hotel
Sadler Gate

With beat groups and R&B bands taking over the dance floors in pubs and hotels, the Old Bell Hotel in Sadler Gate decided to get in on the act. The opening night of its new R&B club on Sunday 27th August 1964 featured The Von-dereras which were given an enthusiastic reception. This confirmed the increasing demand for this genre of music, especially with Derby's new Mod movement. The Bell was one of Derby's oldest and largest coaching inns with a history stretching back 350 years. Over time the building was heavily modified as it changed from a coaching inn to a hotel, bar, restaurant and dance hall. The Old Bell Hotel has numerous ghost stories and tales which have spawned from its history and it was featured on TV shows including *Most Haunted*. One story concerns a former maid named Mabel who was said to have hanged herself in her room after discovering she was pregnant. Another maid was said to have been attacked by one of Bonnie Prince Charlie's soldiers. The introduction of the 1964 R&B club in the Bell's Tudor Ballroom paved the way for it to become a favourite dance and 'live' music venue right up to recent times.

SUNDAY BEAT AT THE BELL

— October 25th —
THE JUNCO PARTNERS
— November 1st —
THE PIGS
— November 8th —
THE JETTS
— November 15th —
THE RAPIDS.

The Windmill Club
The Morledge

Influenced by the success of Jack Holland's Balmoral Club, Rick Moylan, the landlord of the Windmill public house at Breadsall Hilltop, ventured onto the club scene. The Windmill Club was located on land behind the Ice Factory and above garden machinery retailer, Tinkler & Hudson.

It opened in September 1964 and like the Balmoral it catered for the older socialite with a casino, a restaurant and dancing to its resident dance band, the Don Coles Trio. Cabaret nights saw national and local artist performing at the club including the ubiquitous Jazz singer, Mave Pinkney.

Trocadero 1963 - 1965
Normanton Road

Sammy Ramsden spent over three years trying to compete against the mighty Mecca organisation and to cater for the social changes brought on by the shiny new decade. With mixed success The Trocadero struggled on until July 1964 when, at the age of 78, Sammy Ramsden retired and sold the ballroom to the owners of the Silver Blades Ice Rink in Leeds. Soon after that he also sold his Derby home and moved back to his native Lancashire to live out his final years in Blackpool

Demolition of the Trocadero

where he died in July 1968 aged 82. The Trocadero continued as a Bingo Hall well beyond the end of the decade. The building then lay empty for several years until this iconic venue tragically burnt to the ground in October 1982. The site was developed for community housing aptly named Trocadero Court, although many Derbians may have thought that Ramsden's Court would have been more appropriate in recognition of Sammy's colourful character.

Trocadero Court. The name lives on along with the distinctive lime trees

A Tribute to Patrick Shippey
Derby's first independent DJ

I first met Patrick Shippey in late 1962 at one of the lunchtime record sessions at Derby's Locarno ballroom. From my regular position on the balcony, overlooking the twin-deck record console, I had often seen this young West Indian lad bouncing around the ballroom. He usually had a paper bag in his hand and would stop to chat to the some of the regulars and show them the contents of his bag. We soon became good friends because his bag contained rare American vinyl with exotic sounding labels such as Tamla, Vee-Jay and Philles.

At the time, the labels and artists names were unknown this side of the Atlantic, but they sounded so exciting to me: The Marvelettes, Martha & The Vandellas, The Miracles, etc. If I remember rightly, Patrick had told me that his uncle worked on the ships in Liverpool and would return from the USA with gifts of these wonderful 45s. But Patrick didn't sell his precious discs, he would loan them to his friends, perhaps in the interest of his life's mission; to wean us British kids off Mersey Mania and to expand our music tastes to the wonderful R&B and Soul music that was available in the States.

At this time Patrick was already playing his music at parties around Normanton's West Indian community where DJs were called MCs (Masters of Ceremonies).

As the sixties progressed this disciple of soul crossed-over to the white side of town and became one of Derby's most popular and well-respected DJs. His pseudo names included Sir Lees Downbeat 1V, His Worshipful Highness the Duke of Rollo, King Pleasure and Mr Soulful. For a time, I acted as his manager and he would travel with our band to gigs, and play his music during the breaks.

I have so many great stories about Patrick but my favourite was when he was working as a bus conductor in 1969. I was in my office at the Derbyshire Advertiser after it had moved from the Market Place to Trinity Terrace opposite the old Derbyshire Royal Infirmary. It was mid-morning and suddenly Patrick burst into my office. His opening line was something like "Hey man, I've got some great new platters for you". He then unpacked his shoulder bag and spread a selection of American imports over my desk, giving me a short review in the process. Before I could respond he said: "Anyway man, I've got to go now, my bus is outside". I followed him onto the pavement and there stood a stationery number 33 Corporation bus bound for Alvaston with the driver and passengers looking none too pleased. Patrick jumped on the back of the bus, pressed the bell, and swung round the pole as the bus continued its route. It wasn't even a bus stop.

Derby has been blessed with many colourful characters over the years, not people that were rich or famous in the popular sense, but people everyone seemed to know and that became part of the very fabric of the town centre. These characters have become part of Derby's folklore and Patrick Shippey's contribution to the City's social history and music scene puts him among them.

Patrick Shippey was born on May 30th 1944. He died of a long-standing heart condition on April 7th 2020, aged 76.

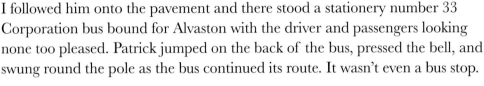
I was there!

The memories of Paul Shippey (aka Shabber) New Zealand, Derby.

Patrick Shippy's son, Paul, an NHS worker at the Royal Hospital, Derby, since 2009, shares his memories. The father of three followed in his father's footsteps and has become a well-known DJ on Derby's soul and reggae music scene.

Dad was born in 1944 in Bog Walk, Jamaica and as a teenager in the early 60s he emigrated to Derby with a handful of records and not much else. That was the start of Patrick Shippey's musical journey. From an early age dad loved all types of music including reggae, blues, R&B, soul, gospel and jazz. Dad had a great knowledge of music from all around the world. He could tell you who sang what, the release date, what label it was on and its highest chart position on both sides of the Atlantic. He built his own sound systems and performed at many birthday parties, weddings, pubs and clubs around Derby and further afield. As a child I remember the coffee table at home was a speaker cabinet and the TV stand a record box. Dad made them all in our living room but he was no joiner. Everything he built was square and there would be sawdust everywhere. Dad had a vast collection of vinyl but no way was I allowed to touch it. He would do sound checks at all hours, even on a school night, but Sundays were the best with dad playing his music while my mum was in the kitchen making dinner. Patrick worked as a 'Clicky' collecting the fares on the old trolleybuses. I remember him swinging from the pole at the back of the bus as it swished up and down Normanton Road. Dad also drove a forklift truck at the at loco works but music was his chosen profession and he was the man-about-town if you needed advice on rare music (preferably vinyl). So, dad helped lay the foundation of the Derby music scene and I am doing my best to follow in his footsteps.

CHAPTER 3: 1966 to 1969
MARCH OF THE MODS

Soul Music and Discos take over the scene

DANCEFLOOR FILLERS

1. ARTHUR CONLEY.
Sweet Soul Music

2. THE CAPITOLS.
Cool Jerk

3. GLADYS KNIGHT & THE PIPS.
Just Walk in My Shoes

4. DONNIE ELBERT.
A Little Piece Of Leather

5. CHUBBY CHECKER.
At The Discotheque

6. SLY AND THE FAMILY STONE.
Dance To The Music

7. JUNIOR WALKER & THE ALLSTARS.
How Sweet It Is

8. BOB & EARL.
Harlem Shuffle

9. CHRIS FARLOW.
Out Of Time

10. PROCUL HARUM.
Whiter Shade Of Pale

Geno Washington and The Ram Jam band at Clouds

In the mid-sixties the Mod movement came to the fore and this exclusive band of stylish kids soon influenced the mass-market. When the Mods 'came back-down' after returning from a weekend at one of the all-nighter clubs in the neighbouring larger cities they wanted somewhere more local to satisfy their music taste. Soul music was their first choice and very soon enterprising individuals arranged events in local clubs and pubs where the Mods could dance the Block, the Jerk, the Duck or do the Monkey. This new sub-culture indirectly gave birth to Derby's Clouds club which became one of the country's leading venues for soul music attracting visitors from miles around.

54

Following this, the club scene started to flourish with new venues popping up around the town. Disc Jockey's had become as popular, and sometimes more popular, than local beat groups and bands. Pubs, clubs, and even private events, often employed a DJ rather than live music.

Throughout 1966 and into 1967, the Mod influenced R&B and Soul venues flourished in Derby and the rest of the UK. Soon afterwards, something else was happening in Europe and the USA which would change the image and offerings of dance venues for the rest of the decade – the Discotheque was born.

Belgium born singer and actress, Regine Zylberberg, who ran clubs in Paris, replaced the juke-box, ubiquitous in French dance venues at the time, with turntables and disc jockeys. This new format, she often said, justified her claim to be "the inventor of the Discotheque." By the mid-60s she had opened several Discos across the world. Regine Zylberberg died on 1st May 2022 aged 92.

The term Discotheque was quickly adopted by every dance venue in the UK, from a bash in the village hall or the local pub to established dance venues and top London clubs. This, in turn, gave birth to the Mobile Disco.

Followers of the Mod movement weren't happy about Discotheques sweeping the nation. After all, the very essence of being a Mod was to be different from the rest of society. On top of that, Mod fashion had also become too commercial and available at most boutiques and even high street multiple fashion retailers. These cultural changes probably contributed to the slow decline of the Mods until a revival took place in the 70s.

The new generation of teenagers joining the scene around 1967 would have been influenced by Flower Power and the Hippy movement, but it wasn't just them. We saw some die-hard Mods trading their parkas and mohair suits for kaftans, beads and bangles and their scooters for Minis – a revolution within a revolution.

TEN TOP DANCES

The Matador

The Block

The Stomp

The Blue Beat

The Hully Gully

The Hitch Hiker

The Duck

The Monkey

The Jerk

The Dog

In addition to soul and pop music, the clubs, discos and DJs hosted more diverse events. Weekend Hippies swayed dreamily to psychedelic sounds with the occasional punter (perhaps under the influence of something) bursting onto the floor to perform a 'Loon Dance' – which perhaps is self-explanatory.

Around this time there was a rise in the popularity of Reggae music which had been alive and kicking all the way through the 60s within West Indian communities. Again, the clubs, discos and DJs responded accordingly by including this genre into their playlists. Soul and Pop Music was mixed with Reggae, Blue Beat and Ska and the dance floors became dominated by the athletic skills of the black dancers.

By the end of the 60s, for some of the young, cool kids in town, the hippy influence had morphed into a harder and more serious genre which they called Heavy Rock or Prog Rock (Progressive Music) which was pioneered by bands like Pink Floyd, The Moody Blues and Led Zeppelin.

At the same time, Derby's original Mods were perhaps becoming too old to keep up their hectic, youthful lifestyle. Many were settling down with girlfriends and getting married, leaving their legacy behind. The Mod movement returned underground only to be resurrected in the 70s by a new generation of Mods which, with help from clubs like the Wigan Casino, gave birth to the Northern Soul genre.

As the decade gradually drew to a close, we also saw an increase in more sophisticated dance venues which targeted the mature socialite and provided cabaret and dining along with music and dancing. The most successful of these was in Colyear Street, The Hippo which opened in 1969 and went on to become the town's most successful club for dancing in the early 70s. But the shiny, brand-new Hippo, sadly, helped close the door on the magical 60s – a decade which had many cultural changes and provided varied, exciting and exhilarating venues for dancing in Derby.

TEN FASHION FAVOURITES
GIRLS
Crepe de chine shift dresses
Mini skirts
Black and white Op Art fabrics
White knee-length socks
White patent leather boots
Skinny-rib sweaters
Dog tooth checked suits
Hot Pants
Vidal Sassoon 5-point hairstyles
Colours: purple, lime green, orange
BOYS
Striped 'Ice Cream' jackets
Desert boots
Made-to-measure Tonik mohair suits
Elephant cord trousers
Roll neck jumpers
Fred Perry shirts
Nylon Macs
Full-length Leather Coats
Hipster flared trousers
Tie-Dyed T-Shirts

Discovery Discotheque
Friargate

By the start of 1966 most Derby teenagers were influenced by the Mod movement. No longer an underground sub-culture, it had become the main influence on a teenager's lifestyle – what to wear, what music to listen to and how to dance.

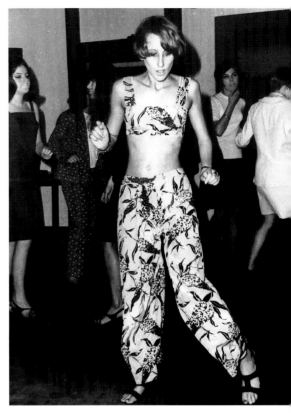

The Corporation Hotel had paved the way with its R&B nights and had become the Mods venue of choice. But their weekend trips to the all-nighter clubs in Manchester, Sheffield and Stoke had left them wanting more. At these out-of-town clubs, rare American soul music on 45rpm vinyl discs was taking over from live bands and, influenced by the discotheque phenomenon which was sweeping Europe and America, the club DJs were becoming the stars.

Together with Jim Milton and Joe Gunther, a couple of well known 'faces' on the Derby scene, we could see an opportunity and decided to open Derby's first ever Discotheque. This decision would eventually lead directly to the opening of perhaps the most iconic dance venue the city has ever known – Clouds.

I had stopped playing in Godfrey's Grit'n'Soul Band to concentrate on this exciting new venture and our first task was to find a venue. Our band used to play at The Wheel Hotel in Friargate (later to be known as The Garrick,

Thirsty Scholar and The Mile) and so I spoke to the landlord who was Derby's first West Indian publican. He agreed to rent the upstairs function room to us every Sunday evening for a few quid a night.

Discovery Discotheque
Friargate

With the help of Patrick Shippy (See pages 52/53) we managed to cobble together a very basic sound system with the record decks mounted on a piano which we draped with a huge Union Jack flag. To create a club atmosphere we replaced all the light bulbs in the wall lights with coloured bulbs.

As I worked for a newspaper, it was my job to place the weekly advertisements for Discovery in the Derby Evening Telegraph. But this was harder than I thought it would be. Before the opening night announcement was published, I received a call from the paper querying the word Discotheque. The typesetter had gone to his boss asking "What's this word 'Discoth-e-queue'.

Where the Action is

DISCOVERY
DISCOTHEQUE CLUB

WEDNESDAYS and SUNDAYS

Members 2/6
Guests 3/-

THE WHEEL, Friargate

Jim Milton was the main DJ with the occasional spot from Patrick (Mr Soulful). As well as the latest Soul and Tamla Motown releases Jim and Patrick managed to get hold of some rare American imports. Joe and I were on the door and charged 2/6d (12.5p) admission. It was an instant success with queues forming right down Friargate each Sunday evening. It became the place to be seen if you were 'in'. Within a matter of weeks, we added Wednesday night sessions which were just as successful and we packed the small upstairs room with hot, sweaty dancers showing off the moves they'd learned at the big city all-nighters.

I remember one evening when we were getting ready to open-up, this young Bemrose school lad turned up and asked Jim if he could help setting up the equipment. He'd seen our advert in the Derby Telegraph and thought it sounded interesting. Jim showed him how the system worked and let him play a few records. His name was Trevor East who was soon to make his name as Derby's most popular DJ.

Because we were part of the Mod crowd who were our paying customers, it created jealousy amongst some of the members. One night while I was taking the entry fee at the top of the stairs, three well know Mod 'hard boys' tried to take over the club at knife point. Trevor heard the commotion and was quick to react. He grabbed the money box and legged it downstairs and out of the building. I don't remember how we pacified the interlopers but normal service was soon resumed.

Patrick Shippey

Trevor East

Joe Gunther

Roger Smith

We knew most of our members but when we weren't sure of their names, Jim and Trev gave them nicknames based on the records they always requested. There was a girl called 'Aint Too Proud To Beg' and one called 'Just Walk In My Shoes'.

Despite its success, Discovery would only last for about six months. The word soon got around and a journalist friend of mine, Phil Baldy, who was a regular at the club, told a friend and local business man, Stan Fowkes, about Discovery. Jim and I were then invited to meet Mr Fowkes at his office across the road from the old Plaza ballroom on London Road.

Within a few weeks of that meeting, Discovery ceased to exist as we moved on to a much more successful project. Our Discotheque had certainly helped pave the way for the iconic Clouds club, but sadly, at the time of writing the historic public house that housed Discovery was being turned into student accommodation.

The memories of Nigel Green, Breadsall Village.

I was there!

I first went to Discovery one Sunday evening in 1966 with friends Trev and Fitz. We were only 15 and not exactly Mods at the time, or that interested in Soul and Motown. But, after going twice a week thereafter, we soon became devotees of both styles of music. My overriding memory of Discovery at the Wheel was this hot, sweaty and poky room with a wooden floor that literally bounced up and down to everyone's dance moves. I'm pretty sure Trevor East was the DJ (quite silent in the early days) along with Jim Milton.

The Clouds
London Road

Friday 2nd December 1966 is a date that will be remembered by many of the teens and twenties who were on Derby's social scene at that time. It was the grand opening of the Clouds club - perhaps the most iconic music and dance venue the city has ever known.

To say that this was an exciting period in a decade of dance in Derby would be an understatement. For those involved with the creation of The Clouds (very quickly referred to as just 'Clouds') it was a case of 'being in the right place at the right time'. First of all, the burgeoning Soul Music-loving Mod movement was at its peak. Then, as mentioned earlier, Discovery Discotheque, which opened earlier that year, had highlighted a potential that couldn't possibly be realised in the small upstairs room of a pub. Finally, it coincided with the formation of a consortium of local businessmen, registered as Cymbal Entertainments Ltd, which had decided to take a lease on the vacant premises of the old Plaza ballroom with the intention of developing a club which would rival anything Derby could offer.

Located on London Road above Sanderson and Holmes, the Rolls-Royce car dealership, the premises had been lying empty since the ballroom closed in 1957 and required extensive redevelopment. The main spokesman in the seven strong consortium was Stan Fowkes who ran an accountancy business. But the consortium member behind most of the venue's redevelopment work was Reg Harris who owned the Derby Joinery & Shopfitting Company. He called upon well-known Derby architect, Derek Montague, to assist with the design work and oversee the development of the project.

As the development plans got under way, a journalist friend, Phil Baldy, told me that an acquaintance, Stan Fowkes, wanted to meet Jim Milton and myself to discuss a business proposition. The outcome of the meeting was an offer to employ both of us to run the new club. Through Phil Baldy, he was aware of the success of Discovery and that we had an influence over a very lucrative market for the new club. The consortium could also see that Jim's DJ skills and knowledge of the music scene could be the key to the new club's success. That was it, Jim left his job at the Tax office and was appointed manager of the club. I wasn't prepared to give up my day job but agreed to look after the marketing and promotion of the club in my spare time and to help out during events at weekends.

Jim Milton

So where did the name Clouds come from? Reg Harris, with his joinery and shopfitting company, was perhaps the man who was most involved with the club's development and his son, Haydn, who was only nine at the time, told me that the naming was all down to his mother. One day, after climbing the two flights of stone stairs to see how the work was coming along, she made a comment along the lines of: "This is a long way up, if we go any further, we'll be up in the clouds". The decision was made and after that I designed and illustrated the first Clouds logo using Letraset and pen and ink.

More memories from Nigel Green, Breadsall Village.

The opening night of Clouds was the most anticipated night of our lives, although not billed as an all-nighter, with a 3am finish, it was the closest thing to anything I had been to. The place was packed to the rafters and we saw our first live soul act - Geno Washington and The Ram Jam Band. Absolute knockout and the first of many to come. Towards the end of the night, I was stopped by several people asking if I was the guy that had put his foot through the ceiling of the stage. Apparently the leg belonged to a member of The Ram Jam Band who was wearing a pair of distinctive, white jeans which is exactly what I was wearing, hence the mistaken identity. Subsequently, I never wore those jeans on a night out again! However, in retrospect, it could have been plaster dust on his leg. One other memory that has stuck with me was when the Showstoppers performed. They hadn't been on for long when there was a police raid, the sound system was switched off and all the lights came on. Although not a regular occurrence, the local drugs squad would pop in from time to time to do a cursory sweep of the place looking for suspicious substances like dope and pills. Before they left, the lead drugs officer stepped on stage and said 'You all came to see the Showstoppers, well you certainly saw them tonight.'

The Clouds
London Road

*Geno opens
Clouds*

The Grand Opening

The opening of Clouds was the talk of the town. Top of the bill was Geno Washington and The Ram Jam Band supported by The Makin Sounds from London's Flamingo Club and TVs *Ready Steady Go* dancers.

The queue was so long that it nearly reached The Spot at the junction with Osmaston Road. This attracted the attention of the police, who ordered the club to close its doors as soon as the 400-attendance limit was reached. At 9.50pm the doors were slammed shut leaving hundreds of revellers locked out. The remaining queue slowly dispersed, hugely disappointed.

Back inside, the atmosphere was electric with chants of 'Geno, Geno' echoing round the club, even while the well-respected Making Sounds was still performing its warm-up set. Between the live performances, Milt James (Jim Milton) and Trevor East performed on the twin-decks.

Geno Washington and his Ram Jam Band certainly didn't disappoint. Their high-tempo, soulful set left the exhausted audience chanting for more, but the drama wasn't over. During Trevor East's closing set of soulful sounds the ceiling above the DJ console collapsed, showering him, his decks and records with 'clouds' of plaster and dust. No, it wasn't part of the show, all eyes on the hole in the ceiling would have seen a swift withdrawal of a dusty human leg, which it is believed, belonged to one of the members of The Ram Jam Band who had found his way up into the roof space to entertain one of the female members of the audience.

That put an end to the music that night and the crowd had to finally come down from the Clouds at 3am and head for home after a truly memorable night.

Besides Mods from across the Midlands helping to create the unique Clouds atmosphere, the club enjoyed a large following of US troops who were based between Burton-on-Trent and Uttoxeter at RAF Fauld. Most of these visitors were black and they couldn't believe that they were able to hear their favourite Blues and Soul music from across the Atlantic. Back home in the USA they probably wouldn't have been able to mix with whites in a venue like Clouds.

THE CLOUDS
LONDON ROAD, DERBY

BIG BILLED, ACTION PACKED
Xmas Programme

| JAZZ SCENE Tuesday Dec. 20th JOHN MAYALL THE BLUES BREAKERS MEMBERS 6/6. GUESTS 7/6 7.30-1.0 | Friday, Dec. 23rd JOHN EVAN SOUL BAND MEMBERS 6/6. GUESTS 7/6—7.30-1.0 |

— CHRISTMAS EVE —
The Shotgun Express
Rod STEWART, Beryl MARSDEN.
Peter BARDENS
MEMBERS ONLY £1. — 8.30-3.0

| Friday, Dec. 30th CHRIS FARLOWE MEMBERS ONLY 12/6 8.0-1.0 | NEW YEARS EVE See the New Year 'in' with the FAMILY MEMBERS ONLY 15s Tickets available |

Monday, January 2nd - AFTERMATH
JIMMY JAMES AND THE VAGABONDS
MEMBERS ONLY 8/6   7.30-11.0

SPEND THIS CHRISTMAS IN THE CLOUDS

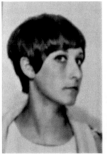

Top: Rholda Wiggett, right, with friend Chris Adams.
Below: The Girls in 2022

I was there!

The memories of Rholda Wiggett, Littleover.

My best friend, Chris Adams, and I were inseparable in those days and when the Clouds opened, we became regulars despite the fact that I was only sixteen. It was like no other club we'd experienced before and besides the great soul music and the fabulous live bands it even had its own hairdressing salon housed in a booth just down from the entrance. I sometimes had my hair done there before the sessions started. Next to this was a booth displaying the latest mod fashions from Derby's top boutique, Napoleon and Josephine, 'Nap and Jo's' as everyone called it. They staged a fashion show at Clouds and we were asked to be models along with Chris's sister Kay, and our friends Lynne Darby and Helen Simms. Chris and I would always dance on the stage to get noticed, perhaps because she fancied one of the black American servicemen who frequented the club. She thought he looked like Harry Belafonte. One of his mates came onto the stage and asked me if the white guy I had been dancing with was my boyfriend. When I asked why, he said 'I would like to dance with you and wanted to make sure it would be allowed in here.' He was so polite and even asked the boy I had been dancing with if it would be ok. We danced, and I remember that he was very tall and was wearing big, lace-up boots that seemed to go half way up his leg. It was probably part of his uniform, but despite that he managed to make some impressive moves.

The Clouds
London Road

Zoot Money at Clouds

The early years

Manager Jim Milton was at the sharp end of running the club. He had developed an extensive knowledge of American Soul music on Leicester's early Mod scene before his family moved up the M1 to Derby in 1964. Not only that, he had been a drummer in one of Leicester's top bands, The Berkeley Squares, alongside Rick Grech who went on to play with Eric Clapton's Blind Faith and Roger Chapman who became part of Family.

In that first year of Clouds, Jim Milton knew exactly which acts to book to attract the target market. He developed a relationship with London's entertainment agencies and was often able to negotiate great deals for up-and-coming stars before their fees rocketed.

Jim was an excellent dancer too. When the Twist became a national craze in 1962, he entered a competition and came second in the London final, the winner of which was a young Mod named Marc Feld who later became Marc Bolan, the singer with T Rex.

I was there!

Bryan Bennion, Spondon.

I was there on the opening night of Clouds in December 1966. Geno Washington and The Ram Jam Band were the main attraction but I'm sure most lads went along to watch the Ready Steady Go dancers who were also on the bill. Soon after that I saw Family with Roger Chapman and after that they couldn't keep me and my friend Rod Patton away. We saw so many big American soul artists there including Ben E King, the Showstoppers, Garnet Mimms and several versions of the Drifters. Whenever I could I would capture them on my Asahi Pentax camara. When we saw the Fabulous Temptations, most people realised they weren't the actual Temptations. They were The Velours who just covered all the Temptations songs. However, they later became The Fantastics and had hits including Baby Make Your Own Sweet Music. Another band that appeared at Clouds were The Vibrations who had hits with My Girl Sloopy and Canadian Sunset. I managed to get back stage to talk with them and when I asked their names, I recognised two of them. So, I asked "Are you Sam Erv and Tom who recorded Soul Teacher?" They were surprised I had heard of them let alone owned the single on an import label. The night Garnett Mimms appeared he only performed for 30 minutes but was outstanding. As he was leaving the stage I asked if he was coming back on again. He said that he was only being paid for that long. So, we had a word with the management and they agreed to pay him more and he played again. Although it ended up being a repeat of the first set it was well worth it.

Garnet Mimms

The Vibrations

The Platters　　*Photos: Bryan Bennion*

So, Jim Milton was without doubt the man for the job. As well as being manager he would even take over on the twin turntables under the name Milt James and brought with him his 'apprentice' from Discover Discotheque - Trevor East. Trevor quickly developed his skills at Clouds and became Derby's most popular DJ for the rest of the decade.

The first 12 months of Clouds were without doubt the most successful and it maintained a huge following from around the region and beyond. Big names taking the stage during that period included The Isley Brothers, Edwin Starr, Rod Stewart, Family, Zoot Money and Chris Farlowe. Even a few, soon-to-be stars, humped their equipment up the stone stairs, including Reg Dwight, keyboard player with Long John Baldry's band Bluesology, who later went solo and changed his name to Elton John.

When negotiating bookings with the London agencies, Jim Milton pulled off his biggest coup when he secured a £50 contract for Procul Harum to appear on 26th May 1967, just a couple of weeks before *A Whiter Shade Of Pale* spent five weeks at No.1 in the charts.

Despite the phenomenal success of Clouds, less than a year after the opening, Jim Milton became frustrated by some 'none-showing' acts, including Lee Dorsey and Mary Wells, as well as poor performances from some of the British bands who were backing the headline stars. Jim's frustrations got the better of him and he resigned late in 1967.

I was there!

The memories of Keith Banks, Alvaston.

I went to the Clouds club for many years, starting in 1966, with the opening night. I remember Geno Washington and The Ram Jam Band appearing and many people being turned away. A friend of mine at the time, a local reporter with Raymond's news agency, Trev East, became the DJ there. The venue was renowned for playing many of the early Motown and Soul records that were eventually known as Northern Soul. On Thursday nights, live bands appeared, some later to become famous. I remember standing in for Trev East (later to have a great career in sports broadcasting with ATV, ITV and Sky Sports) as the DJ on a few occasions, when two now famous artists appeared - Rod Stewart and his band, the Shotgun Express, and Robert Plant, prior to his Led Zeppelin days. The latter part of the 1960s saw the arrival of the Clouds club's most famous DJ, Bobby Childs, who in typical Clouds tradition treated all to brilliant soul music. People visited Clouds from all over the Midlands. It gained a reputation for its music and provided many years of enjoyment for me and my friends.

The Clouds
London Road

Black clouds gathering

A replacement was appointed to take over from
Jim Milton but the subsequent promotion of
'live' artists and bands were often unable to
accommodate viable attendances. It is hard to
pin-point the reason behind the decline in the
club's fortunes at this time, but it was perhaps a
combination of several things. First of all, Jim
Milton would always be a hard act to follow.
Then there was the gradual nationwide change
in popular music culture, with R&B and Soul
music having to compete with Hippy influenced
psychedelic sounds, and, eventually, the more
serious Progressive Rock genre. Also, by this time
some of the town's early Mods, the mainstay
of Clouds early success, were settling down and
were no longer regulars on Derby's social scene.

The Fantastics

Ben E King

Finally, the relatively
small 400 capacity of
the club made it harder
to compete with the larger venues in the region
– the agents and artists followed the money.

The new management and the directors tried
gallantly to stem the tide. They increased the
Disco nights with Trevor East returning for the
occasional session and popular Birmingham DJ,
Bobby Childs, who was a particular favourite
of Soul Music lovers, playing one or two nights
a week.

They reduced the bookings of nationally
known 'live' bands apart from a few ambitious
promotions in 1968 which included The Original
Drifters, The Ronettes, Amboy Dukes, Jo-Jo
Gunn, and Amen Corner. They even arranged
nostalgic return performances by Jimmy James
& The Vagabonds, The Family and P P Arnold
in an effort to revive those magical early days of
Clouds. However, it was unlikely that most of
these promotions covered their costs.

Photos: Bryan Bennion

For a period, Clouds also provided space for a Derby County Supporters Association Clubroom. The Derby Telegraph advertised a 'Social Evening' for Rams supporters on Saturday 30th December 1967 with pre-match and post-match refreshment facilities and a Sunday night New Year's Eve party. It is understood that the Rams new manager Brian Clough and his assistant Peter Taylor attended some of these events along with some of the players.

Clouds regulars in the foyer

To illustrate the obvious change in direction of the Clouds music policy during this time, its New Year's Eve offering on 31st December 1968 was Shag Connors and the Carrot Crunchers, Gloucestershire's answer to The Wurzels.

Reg Harris

Despite these gallant efforts the club was probably still losing money except for nights featuring the popular DJ Bobby Childs. The members of the consortium were slowly jumping ship to get out of their commitment, and the few remaining directors had to shoulder the burden of the overheads and 10-year lease. These included Reg Harris whose company, Derby Joinery & Shopfitting, had invested much more than the rest of the consortium. Mr Harris's company had carried out the initial design and development of Clouds and looked after ongoing maintenance, without full payment for materials or labour. Although he, along with the initial consortium of directors, didn't receive their just reward for creating this iconic club, I know that Reg Harris and his sons, Chris, Mark and Haydn, were proud of the Harris family's part in Derby's social history.

Photos: Bryan Bennion

The Fabulous Temptations

The Showstoppers

The Clouds
London Road

The final curtain

The final managerial appointment was made in 1969 when Peter Martin was appointed manager/promotor who continued to help steady the ship. All-Day Raves were introduced with a great line-up on Sunday 2nd March of Ben E King and Jimmy James & The Vagabonds. Then on Friday 12th December, The Original Drifters accompanied by soul legend Percy Sledge took to the Clouds stage.

The Clouds name remained until the end of the decade and briefly into the next. Almost as a swansong, its final promotion of the 1960s was chart-topping girl group The Ronettes on Sunday 22nd December. But big plans were underway for this famous venue.

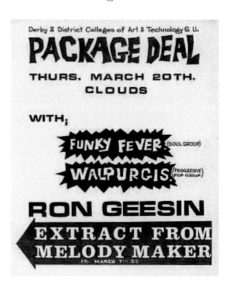

Peter Martin continued in the capacity of manager/promotor into the new decade when Reg Harris instigated a massive interior makeover and the club was re-named Cleopatra's (Cleo's). As they say, 'every 'Cloud' has a silver lining', and this famous dance venue would enjoy a successful revival in the early 70s.

The memories of Bob Chambers, Alvaston (ex-Chaddesden).

I was there!

After leaving Chaddesden's Olive Eden secondary school in 1967 I would later continue to see my old school mates at the youth club there. Our crowd, Steve Darling, Joe Wakefield, Richie Mortimer, Ron Clayton and I, were not too interested in Mersey Beat groups, preferring the Stones, Kinks, Spencer Davis and the Motown artists. We loved playing some recently acquired Soul records at the regular youth club Soul nights. Then a friend of mine, Mick Kavanagh, introduced me to the music of T-Bone Walker and more American Rhythm and Blues, which led me onto further appreciation of Soul music. But I didn't know where I could hear that kind of music in Derby. That was until our crowd discovered Clouds and we soon became regulars. We were all about 17 years old at the time but that didn't stop us starting the evenings with a few pints of Watneys Red Barrel at the infamous Mouse Trap bar at the Cheshire Cheese or the Green Dragon near The Spot. We'd climb up the stone staircase to Clouds feeling 'the bee's knees' in our Levi Jeans and Ben Sherman shirts. And after each step, the exciting soul sounds played by DJ Bobby Childs, would become clearer and clearer. We saw some great acts there including Jimmy James & The Vagabonds and later the Elgins. At the end of the evening when the wonderful sounds ceased and it was time to carefully descend the steps we would sometimes end up at Greasy Pete's, as we called it, a Greek restaurant opposite the Derbyshire Royal Infirmary. The restaurant wasn't licensed but after our meal the old lady waitress would always ask us if we fancied a drink. She would then disappear into the back and return with glasses of beer. Then it was the long walk back to Chaddesden, totally satisfied with the music we'd heard and the food and alcohol we'd ingested.

Clouds officially closed on Sunday 29th August 1971 and Cleopatras opened for business on 8th October 1971. Just before the name change, local promotor, Paul Conway, had successfully relocated his Magic of Ju-Ju, Progressive Rock nights to Clouds, and subsequently Cleo's. The new Cleopatra's club also played a big part in the popularity of the new Northern Soul genre which helped this famous dance venue to establish itself as the shining light on Derby's 'alternative' music scene.

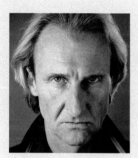

Extracts from the final Clouds review of the 60s from Derby Evening Telegraph Saturday Page Editor, Roy Hollingworth, on 20th December 1969.

Atmosphere of goodness at Arts Ball

It was extremely dark, and the air hung around like matt black stout, pungent, loud and wicked. The Hunchback of Notre Dame hobbled across a wall, and a band played music. In corners, huddles of clouded people sipped and spoke, and laughed. A man with a snap-brim black hat pretended to rob the barmaid, but she shot him dead with an imaginary gun. It was the Derby Art College Ball.

Art College Balls always produce some inexplicable atmosphere of goodness, and Thursday night at the Clouds Club possessed such a quality. People were wearing just what they wanted to, and their hair was long, fuzzed and mean. They sat on the floor, walked around, danced when the music became frenzied. I had a conversation with a very pretty girl, about how good the Clouds was when it was full of something apart from those other sorts of music (soul, reggae, riggi, jiggi, and suchlike), and then East of Eden took the stage, and all was very quiet. Squatting lazily on the floor, the audience truly appreciated the sound, and clapped loud and sincerely.

Next came CHARGE, the band with ever-growing wisdom from the Art College. Their music was accompanied by a strange set of films, which shined behind them and depicted tales of Quasimodo, and other such laughable horrors. Seldom have I seen such real enthusiasm for a local band.

Art Balls don't die, they just fade away, and this one petered out slowly and magnificently. The air was crisp and cold outside, and it had been a fair evening. They always are.

Author's note:

My dear old friend, Roy Hollingworth, was Saturday Page editor of the Derby Evening Telegraph from the late 60s until, in early 1971, he landed a job on Britain's famous weekly music newspaper, Melody Maker. It wasn't long before the MM appointed him New York Correspondent where he spent a few years working and socialising with top British stars including David Bowie and John Lennon. A frustrated musician himself, Roy returned to his home town Derby in 1974 before moving to London where he became a guitar tutor and recorded a CD of his own songs, which sold well, especially in Germany. Roy died on 9th March 2002 aged 52.

The Locarno 1966-1969
Babington Lane

With the slow decline of the Mod movement the Locarno became more popular again and was clawing back patrons from The Corporation and Clouds. It was also capitalising on the universally popular Disco craze, and with its 1,000-capacity limit, was able to compete with Clouds when it came to presenting big money, 'live' artists and bands.

Managers of the Locarno ballroom during the period from 1966 included Harry Fogwell, Bill Gavin and David Havell with resident bands, The Johnny O'Rourke Showband, The  Dave Allen Band, The Jerry Vincent Trio, Jack Jay and his Band, The Bob Snowdon Trio, and in 1969, The Mike Miller Set. Derby's own Alan Rogers Trio would often be called on to provide holiday relief for the resident bands.

During this period the Locarno's famous revolving stage was graced by new supergroup, Cream, which consisted of bassist Jack Bruce, guitarist Eric Clapton, and drummer Ginger Baker. Other big acts included The Tremeloes, the Fantastics, US girl group The Flirtations *(Nothing But A Heartache)*, The Move, Edwin Starr, The Equals and Lee Dorsey.

At the same time, the Locarno still catered for the traditional ballroom dancing enthusiasts with its Over 21 Nights on Wednesdays and Mondays.

The ballroom's Festive Programme was still a big draw and on Christmas Eve 1966 it included an all-day event from midday until midnight which was billed as 'Big Beat Around the Clock - Your last Tuesday disc date for Swinging 1966'.

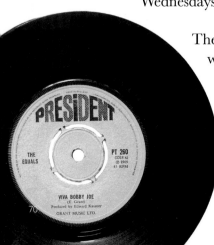

70

Although the Locarno did its best to attract the Mods to its ballroom with appropriate playlists from its resident DJs, and by presenting suitable national and international 'live' artists, they probably left it a bit late. Also, as Clouds had found, besides Ballroom Dancing, Rock'n'Roll, Pop, Rhythm & Blues and Soul, the teens and twenties were becoming divided by more diverse music genres including Psychedelic Rock, Blues Rock, Prog Rock, Folk Rock, Ska and Reggae. Therefore, it became difficult for a large venue like the Locarno to present a programme of events that would be financially viable and would suit all.

The Locarno had tried to deal with changes to its programme by introducing 'Kaleidoscope Disco Club' on Sundays. Then 'Thoroughly Mod Friday's' were introduced but these were cancelled on 2nd August 1968 - a sign that the Mods were in retreat. They even gave a nod to the Hippys with 'Freak Out' on 30th December 1966 starring The Mike Cotton Sound plus US Singing Star, Lucas.

The memories of Gareth Butler, California, USA

I was born in South Wingfield, Derbyshire, and after leaving Swanwick Grammar School I had a few half-hearted attempts at finding a suitable career option. Then I discovered a vacancy for a DJ at Derby's Locarno Ballroom. I'd always been interested in the pop music of the day so I applied and the manager, Dave Havell, gave me the job. My stage name was simply 'Gary' which was emblazoned on the back of my bright red stage jacket. I loved my job and would appear via the famous revolving stage to the sound of Arthur Conley's, Sweet Soul Music. Once I found my feet I introduced 'The Locarno Line-Up'. This was a weekly countdown of the most requested records which I would play, in turn, from No.10 right up to No.1, which I would introduce with a dramatic fanfare. The kids loved it. But my spell at the Locarno would only last just over a year. My best school friend, Phil Hallam, was planning to emigrate to Canada and he persuaded me to join him. Commercial radio was so big on the other side of the Atlantic and I fancied my chance as a Radio DJ. It was a decision I had to make in a hurry and so I had to break the news 'live' to my Locarno audience. After my announcement I was suddenly drenched with the contents of a pint of beer. My girlfriend at the time was on the balcony with an empty glass in her hand and looking very angry. It was the first time she had heard about my plans. I DJ'd in some of the best clubs in the Toronto area until I landed a job on Chum radio. But my plans for a career on Canadian radio were short lived when they told me that their audience were having difficulty understanding my broad, Derbyshire accent.

The Locarno 1966-1969
Babington Lane

In November 1969, manager Dave Havell announced a complete change to The Locarno's musical presentation. Gone were the nine-piece band, gone were the Trio, and a new outfit would take over as Five and Fitz, a five piece band with two girl singers. Local Repton DJ, Yvette took over on the turntables.

Godfrey's Grit'n'Soul Band

Despite these attempts to cater for all, The Locarno was still the venue of choice for private annual events. In June 1967 Pink Floyd topped the bill at the Rolls-Royce Apprentice Ball with an early line-up which included Syd Barrett, Roger Waters, Rick

Wright and Nick Mason. On 22nd December 1967, Derby Students Union presented The Alan Price Set, Sons & Lovers and John Smith Affair, all supported by the ubiquitous DJ Trev East. And on Friday 28th March 1969 The Art and Technical College Students Union presented a 'Caribbean Ball' featuring British-based USA vocal group The Fantastics (Something Old, Something New). A steel band also performed and ticket holders were encouraged to wear Hawaiian style dress.

The Alan Rogers Trio

But big changes were on the horizon. An almost prophetic promotion took place in September 1969 when lovers of traditional ballroom dancing were invited to a nostalgic evening to relive the halcyon days of the Big Band when The Syd Lawrence Orchestra presented a programme of music made famous by Glen Miller.

The change in popular social culture wouldn't have been confined to Derby and a similar dilemma would have affected Mecca ballrooms across the country. Bizarrely, in December 1968 the Locarno suddenly became known as La Locarno, but their strategy relating to this change remains a mystery. Perhaps it was a desperate corporate decision by Mecca to refresh its brand image. However, this name change was short lived and, just as Clouds had plans for a radical change, in May 1970 the Locarno would be relaunched as Tiffany's after a massive interior refit.

It seemed that owners of dance venues felt the need to leave the Swinging 60s behind to keep up with the times and embrace the new decade with radical changes.

On 20th December 1969 'La' Locarno celebrated its 10th anniversary with music from the Mike Miller Set, which was rather low-key billing to celebrate the history of such an iconic venue. But the writing was on the wall and, once again, another famous name would disappear from Derby's social scene. A name synonymous with dancing in Derby, and a name that will last in the memories of so many.

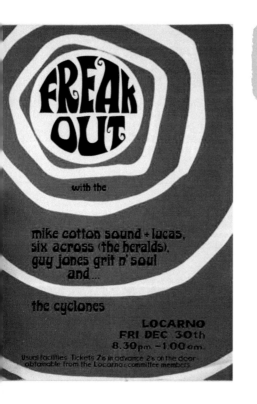

FREAK OUT

with the

mike cotton sound + lucas, six across (the heralds), guy jones grit n' soul and...

the cyclones

LOCARNO
FRI DEC 30th
8.30pm - 1.00 am.
Usual facilities Tickets 7/6 in advance 2/6 on the door obtainable from the Locarno committee members

I was there!

The memories of Hilary Slater (nee Bennett), Repton

Whenever I think of the Locarno there is one night that always comes to mind. I was about 17-years old and at one of the mid-week Disco nights that would attract some of Derby's fashionable Mods. I was with my friend, Gwendoline Grundle, and we were both wearing halter-neck backless dresses that my mum had made for us. Mine was black, Gwen's was blue and we felt really good. We were dancing near the stage and I noticed that a boy was watching us. As soon as we retreated to the side of the dancefloor, he came over to me and asked: "Do ya want ta dance?" He was dressed like an old teddy boy, wearing a suit with tight trousers, crepe sole shoes and white socks. He was even sporting a Brylcreemed quiff. I politely said "No thank you." But as I turned away with my nose in the air he shouted: "What do ya expect for five bob duck, James Bond?" Well, his response floored me. Not only did I find it hilarious but it made me question my own prejudice. So, I turned back and danced with him. I think we were dancing to Gene Pitney's 'Twenty Four Hours From Tulsa'. But his time only lasted about three minutes.

The Balmoral 1966-1969
Charnwood Street

Jack and Winifred Holland

The Swinging 60s was at its peak in 1966 and The Balmoral Club was still operating successfully as a sophisticated venue for more mature members.

Buoyed by his success, Jack Holland had expanded his organisation by turning the old Cosmo cinema in Upper Boundary Road into Dino's Cabaret Club. He didn't stop there, taking over the running of the Rialto Ballroom and renaming it The Stork Club.

Jack Holland's Central Estates property business was also still operating successfully and he was clearly 'on-a-roll', as they say. But his nose for a business opportunity was truly tested in 1967 when an acquaintance popped into Jack's office. Aware of Jack's love of the Bahamas, he made him aware of how the islands were developing into international holiday hot-spots for the rich and famous and that there was money to be made. Despite the success of his Derby operations, Jack, recognised that in the Bahamas his valuable experience in property and hospitality could be put to good use. So, he moved his family there, leaving his 19-year-old son Anthony to complete the sale of his clubs and join them later.

I was there!

More memories from Bridie Flood, Alvaston

I loved working at the Balmoral for the Holland family with the chance to wear glamorous clothes and meet a few celebrities. I remember when pop-star Marty Wild was performing there, he stood behind my blackjack table and, looking down my low-cut dress, said 'You don't get many of those to the pound'. I worked at the Balmoral right up until it closed in 1968 and I can honestly say that my life then and now has been full of fun and laughter.

Young Anthony moved into accommodation above the Balmoral club in Charnwood Street and he continued to run the club until a buyer was found. Within a few months two businessmen from Birmingham made an acceptable offer and paid a 10% deposit. Anthony was left to manage the club while the new owners booked the cabaret acts and looked after the finances. But very soon problems arose, the artist's agents were contacting Anthony to say some acts had not been paid for their appearances. Despite referring them to the new owners, the matter wasn't resolved and one comedian drove to the club and threatened Anthony with a gun. Enough was enough, the club was closed in September 1968 and Anthony joined his family in the apparent luxury and safety of the Bahamas.

That was the end of the Balmoral, one of Derby's most iconic clubs which provided memorable nights out for thousands of members in a style that hadn't been seen in the town before then.

Jack Holland ran several businesses in the Bahamas including a fishing charter where he went under the name of 'Captain Jack'. But the politics on the islands became an obstacle and the family returned to Derby in 1972. Jack died in 2006 at the age of 84 and, at the time of writing, his 98-year-old wife Winifred, son Anthony, and daughter Jill, still live in the city.

Captain Jack' (right) with a satisfied customer

Corporation Hotel 1966-1969
Cattle Market

The Corporation continued with its popular Friday R&B nights but the opening of Clouds in December 1966 soon put paid to that. Having galvanised the Mods into making it their venue of choice the Corporation soon lost their custom. However, its Tuesday's Jazz Club not only continued, but went on to present some of the country's top names including Acker Bilk, Alex Welsh, Terry Lightfoot, George Chisholm and Ken Colyer. Friday's became Folk nights until it was announced that the Hotel was to be demolished to make way for Derby's new inner ring road.

The Grooms

The final Corporation Jazz session took place on Tuesday 30th of December 1969 when Acker Bilk's band brought the curtain down on this iconic music venue. It finally closed in February 1970 and for a short while Derby Jazz Club moved to the neighbouring Windmill Club until that too surrendered to road development.

Thanks to Roger Groom and wife, Mary, the Corporation Hotel became an important part of Derby's popular culture for an entire decade. It played host to the town's music-loving population where they drank and danced many a memorable

Acker Bilk

night away. After the Corporation closed, Roger Groom ran a bookmakers shop in Stable Street until he retired.

The last words came from my friend Roy Hollingworth who wrote in his Derby Telegraph Saturday Page: "Like a faithful dog being horribly killed, we lose The Corporation."

Sherwood Foresters Hotel
St Thomas Road/Village Street, Normanton

Dave Hagues and John Painter's popular Rhythm Club at the Sherwood Foresters Hotel was still running at the start of 1966. It continued to present a programme of local beat groups and R&B bands every Sunday. Around this time the two promotors were also acting as entertainment agents, booking local bands to perform at other venues including the Rialto and Stork Club. The first-floor function room was also a favourite with fans of traditional ballroom dancing and, during the early part of this period, the Sherwood Foresters Hotel regularly presented events featuring local dance bands. But in 1968 this popular venue was forced to close due to new fire safety regulations. After necessary refurbishment the hotel re-opened and continued as a popular public house. The first-floor venue was also available for private one-off functions and a group of young local lads fancied themselves as promotors. They presented two DJs and a 'live' group and ended up with a 'full house.' In 1969 The Sherwood was also home for the Druids Folk Club.

Originally built as a grand, residential hotel, business for the Sherwood Foresters became unviable due to its overhead costs and this historic building lost its sparkle, and its trade. However, it still stands today after being restored to its former glory, as a Sikh temple.

The former Sherwood Foresters Hotel in 2022

Alan Grimadell (left) with Roger Morton from Our Dog Winston

I was there!

The memories of Alan Grimadell, Allestree

I was around fifteen years old when pop music and girls became an important part of my life. Growing up in Allenton in the mid-60s, my mates and I were influenced by the Mod scene in Derby and would make numerous trip to Clouds, the Locarno and the Stork Club. But we also had a great venue almost on our doorstep. We were able to walk to the Sherwood Rhythm Club on Sunday nights to see local beat groups. Two of my mates were budding DJs and another, Roger Morton, played in the group 'Our Dog Winston.' So, we thought we had suitable credentials to promote our own night at the Sherwood. The landlord, Dan Beal, gave us a Friday night slot early in 1968 which we advertised as 'Two Top DJs plus Group'. The only equipment we had was a Dansette record player which we managed to connect to the group's PA system, but the night was still a huge success. The place was so packed that we had to turn people away, although that didn't stop some punters climbing up the drain pipe to get through an open, first-floor window. Fortunately, we didn't lose anyone but we did find some female admirers and ended the night at an impromptu after-gig party somewhere. I do believe that the whole experience was the catalyst for my early career in the 70s working in Hospital Radio and promoting events at the Talk of the Midlands and other venues around Derby.

The Rialto/The Stork Club – 1966 - 1969
Nightingale Road

At the start of this period the Rialto was still presenting local and nationally known artists, rock groups and blues bands. Despite stiff competition from other local venues, it presented an extensive, and expensive, programme of big names. For followers of chart acts these included Heinz (Just Like Eddie), The Move, The Mojos, Alan Price and Georgie Fame. To satisfy the more selective Mod movement, names included Ginger Baker, American R&B legend Irma Thomas, Artwoods, and the High Numbers (later to become Who). Graham Newton, guitarist with 60s local group Six Across, remembers seeing Chris Farlow and The Thunderbirds at the Rialto which at the time included the legendary guitarist, Albert Lee. He told me that his life was never quite the same after that.

REGAL
ZONOPHONE
45 r.p.m.
RZ 3001
FLOWERS IN THE RAIN
THE MOVE

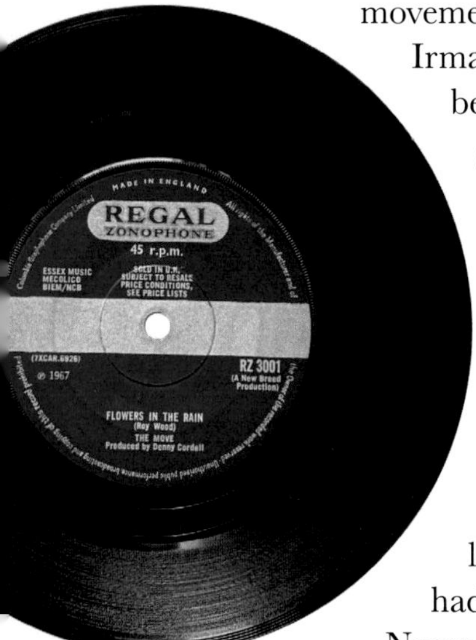

As Clouds had experienced later in the 60s, speculating on booking big named acts with their big money fees was a risky business. This could have contributed to the eventual sale of this famous Derby dancehall and by May 1967, Balmoral Club owner Jack Holland had taken over the Rialto. Never to miss an opportunity, he quickly renamed it The Stork Club which was perhaps a name more appropriate to the time. It also reflected Mr Holland's background in the wining, dining, and cabaret type venues. But sadly, another famous name, Rialto, had disappeared from the town's social scene.

The new Stork Club quickly undercut local pub prices, re-introduced the venue's popular Tuesday Folk Nights, and introduced regular mid-week wrestling events. The Friday Beat Nights were retained and Formal Dancing was introduced on Saturday's featuring the Billy Joyce Trio.

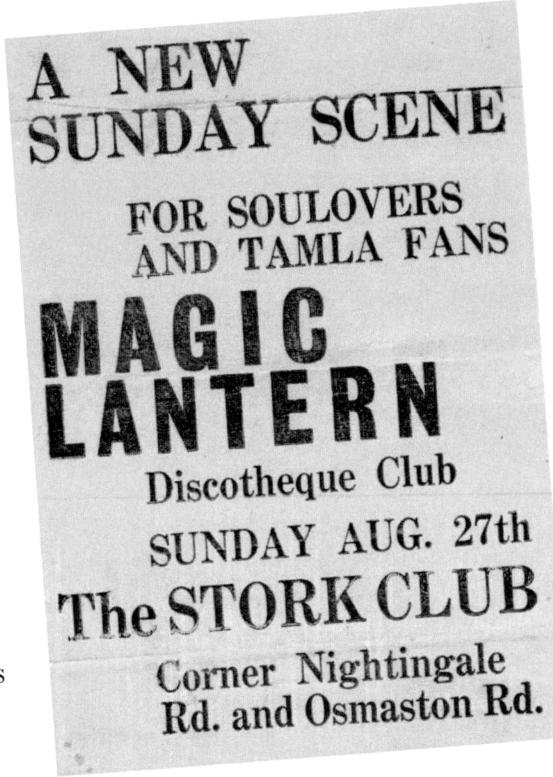

A NEW
SUNDAY SCENE
FOR SOULOVERS
AND TAMLA FANS
MAGIC
LANTERN
Discotheque Club
SUNDAY AUG. 27th
The STORK CLUB
Corner Nightingale
Rd. and Osmaston Rd.

Soon after Jim Milton parted company with Clouds he started the Magic Lantern Discotheque Club at the Stork Club which ran for a few weeks. But Jim had bigger plans and soon left town to pursue business interests in London, initially as a DJ and eventually by opening the Red Records chain of record stores. This opened the door for the final piece in the Stork Club line-up – Shotgun Discotheque. The Sunday night sessions featured Trevor East, who had established himself as Derby's most popular DJ, with me looking after the business side of things. We rented the venue each night and ran it successfully until the club was raided by police for breaching Sunday licensing laws. (More about this later in the Shotgun story)

SEE THE NEW YEAR 'IN'

This Sunday
WITH THE SCINTILLATING
SENSATIONAL SOUNDS OF

SHOTGUN

DISCOTHEQUE

NON-STOP GOODIES

from 8. p.m-12.45 a.m.

THE STORK CLUB

Nightingale Road, Derby,
Members Only; Guests admitted only if accompanied by a member
309c

So, Jack Holland's ideas weren't focussed on dancing and it seems as though he was trying to present a wide variety of entertainment options for all ages and all social sets. But, if so, this strategy must not have paid off because in early 1968 Jack had been tempted by the prospect of greater opportunities in the Bahamas. He quickly sold all his entertainment interests in Derby and took his family off to the West Indian island.

The Stork Club continued operating with either new owners or new management and a much reduced programme of events. After their Sunday sessions ceased following the police raid, Shotgun Discotheque returned in September 1967 and later invited its followers to 'See the New Year In' dancing to 'Non-Stop Goodies'.

From 1969 until the end of the decade, there is little evidence of other regular activities involving dance apart from the occasional private function. So, this famous venue gracefully faded away into Derby's social history.

King's Hall
Queen Street

After The Black Cat Club had moved to the Central Hall, the King's Hall continued to promote nights featuring local and national pop groups. Also, during this period, each year the venue presented a programme of traditional Festive Balls. These events on Christmas Eve and New Year's Eve targeted lovers of ballroom dancing that would feature local dance bands.

Promotions included a line-up of local groups entitled 'Blast Out 66' featuring The Ensigns, The Cyclones, Peppers Machine and The Silhouettes. Then, almost at the end of this period, the King's Hall brought back to Derby the popular Soul Music act, Geno Washington and the Ram Jam Band, the act that performed three years earlier at the opening of Clouds in December 1966.

After the end of the 60s the King's Hall went on to become popular with Progressive Rock fans, competing directly with Magic of Ju Ju at Clouds and Cleopatras. The big names that went on to perform over the boarded-over swimming pool included Genesis, Mott The Hoople and Uriah Heap.

> — TONIGHT —
> KING'S HALL
> DERBY
> Hand Clappin'
> Foot Stompin'
> Funky Butt ....
> LIVE
> GENO WASHINGTON
> and the
> RAM JAM BAND
> Supported by
> ROADRUNNER GO-GO
> and
> GEORGE "DYNO" REED
> 7.30 - 11.30 :: Admission 8/6

Albion Restaurant
Albion Street

Frankie Vaughan meeting fans on an earlier visit to Derby after a performance at the Gaumont Cinema

In the late 60s, Derby Co-op opened the Albion Restaurant in Derby town centre above its new supermarket on Albion Street. Besides operating as a restaurant, offering breakfasts, morning coffee, lunches, and afternoon tea, it became more popular as a function facility. The Albion promoted regular cabaret and dinner/dances presenting many national TV stars including Bob Monkhouse, Dick Emery and Joe Brown and the Bruvvers.

A typical programme advertised in the Derby Evening Telegraph on Friday 2nd August 1968 offered Dinner, Dance and Cabaret for 35/- (£1.75) featuring the glamorous floor show: Barry Young and Les Girls. And on Friday 4th to 7th September: The Frankie Vaughan Show. For Derby's younger dancers, in May 1969, it announced regular Thursday Disco nights which featured Roadrunner and Shotgun Discotheques.

Havana Club
Uttoxeter New Road

Derby's first West Indian Club was opened in 1964 by Solomon Walters (aka Ricky) in the old office premises of the Trent Motor Traction Company. By 1966 it had established itself as one of the country's leading clubs of its kind, attracting coachloads of visitors from Nottingham, Birmingham, Leicester, Manchester, and even as far as London. The Havana was famous for serving up an extensive catalogue of West Indian Reggae music, via the record decks of its resident DJ (or "Master of Ceremonies") who went under the name of Count Campbell (aka Loydi).

On occasions, other out of town DJ's would visit the Havana bringing their own sound systems and collection of rare imported 45rpm vinyl to take part in a friendly competition with Count Campbell and his offerings.

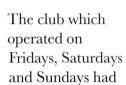

THE HAVANA CLUB
1 UTTOXETER NEW ROAD,
Tel.: 43641
Presents for your Christmas Entertainment

FRIDAY NIGHT
By Popular Demand –
KEENE & HIS BAND
(From Birmingham)
Members 4/-, Guest 6/- (Including Dinner Vouchers)

SATURDAY (Christmas Eve)
Dance to the Music of :–
"COUNT CAMPBELL"
(Derby Top Disc Jockey).
Members 3/6, Guest 5/6 (Including Dinner)

MONDAY & TUESDAY
— THE —
SENSATIONAL SOUND
(from the West). D. J. Cooper.

Spend your Christmas in 'Havana'.

The club which operated on Fridays, Saturdays and Sundays had an official capacity of 200, but would often almost double this number of revellers on Saturday nights, especially when 'live' Reggae bands would perform. The club's upstairs room was popular with the older members of the West Indian Community, but it was the main downstairs dance floor that created the Havana's unique, joyful atmosphere.

The Havana continued to operate successfully well into the following century, but eventually the premises owners, Trent Motor Traction, took the decision to put this famous venue into the hands of a demolition contractor.

An oil and mixed media image on canvas adapted from a photograph by an unknown photographer. In 2022 this was used to promote Derby Museums exhibition: Derby West Indian Community Association: Culture and Legacy.

81

The New Penny
St Peter's Steet

In 1968, the UK was preparing itself to change its pounds, shillings, and pence currency to decimalisation. Although this didn't take place until February 1971, the press was full of it. This, no doubt inspired the name behind Derby's new club, The New Penny Restaurant and Disco, which opened at the back-end of 1968. The entrance was via the arcade which ran between the shop windows of men's tailors, Hepworths, in St Peter's Street.

Its opening advertisements promoted Saturdays as the 'Big Night Out' with music, dancing, and supper included. Its programme for the rest of the week promoted 'Top groups' on Mondays, a 'Teenage Disco' on Tuesdays and Thursdays, and 'Over 21 Night' on Wednesdays.

In 1969 it introduced the New Penny Sunday Club, encouraging Derby's young dancers to apply for membership and "Join the 'In' crowd".

It seems as though the club's aim was to attract Derby's more sophisticated socialites. However, it handed one of its less successful nights over to a local, budding promotor who started something which appeared to eclipse the rest of its programme - Magic of Ju Ju took over Wednesday nights.

Magic of Ju-Ju at The New Penny
St Peter's Street

Paul Conway, the young owner of a newsagents shop around the Abbey Street area, was a big fan of the more serious rock groups and super groups which led to the music genre Progressive Rock (Prog Rock). Paul's newsagent shop specialised in underground magazines such as Oz, International Times and Zig Zag and he was frustrated by the fact that there were few opportunities to see these underground bands in the immediate area.

MAGIC OF JU-JU
UNDERGROUND
BLUES SCENE
O P E N S
WEDNESDAY, SEPTEMBER 17th
— at —
THE NEW PENNY
St. Peter's Street, Derby.
GOOD SOUNDS GUARANTEED
Admission 2/6, 8 p.m.-1 a.m.
WEAR WHAT YOU WANT!
Music, Films, Bring Records if
you like.
Everyone is welcome at the—
MAGIC OF JU-JU

In 1969 he decided to take matters into his own hands and find a venue which would enable him to bring Prog Rock bands to Derby. At that time, the New Penny was perhaps unable to make every night of the week profitable, and he was able to rent the club every Wednesday.

The first Magic of Ju Ju event was on Wednesday September 17th 1969. Two weeks later, the first live band, Tuesday's Children, appeared on stage.

But, by the end of 1969 it became impossible to meet the demand at this small venue and Paul Conway's Magic of Ju Ju nights re-located to Clouds early in 1970 where it continued from strength to strength.

I was there!

The memories of Brian (Sid) Lloyd, Chaddesden

I'll never forget a very special night at the New Penny Club above Hepworths in St. Peter's Street. It was here that, for the first time, Derby opened its doors to its first venue for Rock music. An unlikely location above the retailers of very smart 3-piece suits. This memorable night was Wednesday September 17th 1969; before this the club promoted Soul and Pop Music nights. A new DJ took to the record decks playing rock music under the banner of Magic of Ju-Ju Underground Blues Scene. People were encouraged to bring their own records with the prospect of them being played. Two weeks later the first live band, Tuesday's Children, appeared and the entrance charge was five shillings (25p) which included two slices of cheese on toast, nice! I continued to be a Ju-Ju follower after it moved to Clouds. Some of my favourite bands to appear in subsequent months were Hawkwind, known best for their single Silver Machine, The Groundhogs, Genesis, Climax Chicago Blues Band, Skid Row, Gracious, and Smile, the latter included in its ranks Brian May and Roger Taylor before Freddie Mercury joined and they became Queen.

Club Italia
Osmaston Road

Derby ice cream mogul, Nicola Franco, purchased a grand residential property in Osmaston Road, opposite Bateman Street, mainly because it had extensive rear gardens. At the same time, he had the idea of turning the building into a social club for his fellow Italians who had made Derbyshire their home after the Second World War.

The Club Italia and Ristorante La Gondola building before further redevelopment

One of Mr Franco's associates, Bob Giovannelli, obtained permission from the Italian Embassy to use the name Club Italia and after extensive renovation the club opened in the mid-60s. Although its members were mainly Italian nationals, in 1968 the club's committee made the decision to open it up to the whole town and it quickly became a favourite dance venue. Bob Giovannelli, who ran the club, put together a programme of promotions which included 'live' bands and, with the help of two friends, Sunday Disco nights. His friends, Dave Tice, who had made his name as one of Derby's top Rock'n'Roll dancers, and Mike O'Neil, eventual owner of a successful chain of lighting stores, were the club's DJs.

At the end of the decade, after further re-development, the venue became Ristorante La Gondola with hotel accommodation and function suites, and in the early 70s became Derby's most popular hotel and Italian restaurant.

Bob Giovannelli

Shotgun Discotheque

From 1966 dancing to dance bands and pop groups were on the wane in favour of DJs spinning 45rpm records. The term Discotheque was quickly being adopted by dance venues across the UK which, in turn, gave birth to the Mobile Disco. A result of this was that the DJs themselves became the choice of night-out rather than the venue.

In 1967 Trevor East and I formed Shotgun, probably Derby's first mobile discotheque. We were able to secure residencies at established venues, rent venues for our own promotions and play at one-off private parties. I acted as manager and Trevor was the 'star' performer, having already established himself as Derby's most popular DJ. Our most successful weekly promotion started in the summer of 1967 at the Stork Club. The Shotgun Sunday soul sessions were an instant success until the Police raided it on 29th October 1967 following reports of a breach in Sunday licensing laws. Under the license in those times, entry was restricted to 'Members Only.' I was on the door taking the money when, half-way through the evening, dozens of police officers charged up the stone steps. They guarded the exit to prevent people entering or leaving and instructed Trev to stop playing his records. Officers then proceeded to interview the attendees to establish whether they were members or not. Once interviewed their hands were stamped with red ink.

Whether it's a 'Sock-it-to-me' Party, or a Sophisticated Soiree, Shotgun Discotheque will help you to make a success of your Party, Dance, Reception etc.

SHOTGUN discotheque

7, LAVENDER ROW, DARLEY ABBEY, DERBY **TEL: 57017**

Several visitors on the night were summoned to give evidence at the resulting Court Case to establish whether they were members or not. When one young Mod took to the witness stand the prosecutor asked "And how did you gain access to the premises?" The witness seemed confused by the question, hesitated, and replied, "Er, through the door like everyone else."

Trevor East was underage at the time of the raid and wasn't interviewed because he had been ordered to stay behind his turntables. And ironically, during the court case he was in the press box reporting on the case for his new employers, Raymonds news agency.

I was there!

The memories of Herbie Robinson, Stenson Fields.

I was born in Montego Bay, Jamaica, where I learnt to dance to great Reggae music. In 1964 when I was 17, my family moved to Britain along with my little brother, Judson. But we both soon made names for ourselves on the Derby scene at Clouds, and then Shotgun Discotheque, wherever they played. What we found surprising as new arrivals on the scene, was that it was mainly groups of girls on the dancefloors with the lads just hanging round the bars. I soon changed all that! I had no inhibitions and would join the girls to show-off my moves. In fact, whenever the evenings were slow to get started, Trev East would shout down the mic, 'Herbie, get on the dance floor and let's get things started.' I didn't follow Mod fashions in those days and my signature item was a white jacket which made me easy to spot. Of course, there were many other great black dancers around including my old friend Val Lawrence who was probably better than me. And, white guys became good dancers too, but I like to think that I influenced them in some way.

Dom Polski/The Polish Centre
Osmaston Road and then Kedleston Road

Just as there were many Italian families that made Derby and Derbyshire their home after World War Two, a large contingent of Polish nationals settled in the area. They too, had their own social club, Dom Polski, which was situated on Osmaston Road at the top end of Bradshaw Street (now Bradshaw Way).

After the success of Club Italia, Bob Giovannelli approached the Polish club and persuaded them to let him run a Discotheque there on Sunday evenings. Derby's young dancers responded in good number but soon afterwards the Dom Polski committee decided to move to larger, more prestigious premises on Kedleston Road, near the Five Lamps.

The club then took over management of its own promotions for private functions and public dancing. Throughout 1969 the club, simply renamed The Polish Centre, ran Sunday sessions, often featuring Shotgun Discotheque's DJ, Trev East, Steve Dooley and Colt 45 Discotheque.

Hippo Night Club and Speakeasy
Colyear Street

Towards the end of the decade there were signs that the style of Derby's dance venues was about to change. The new, younger social set weren't that interested in the intimate atmosphere of the independent clubs like Clouds or the Corporation. This was highlighted with the grand opening of the Hippo Night Club and Speakeasy in Colyear Street late in 1969.

The Hippo was a larger and smarter venue offering much more than just music for dancing. Its advertising boasted: 'Derby's No.1 Night Spot for the sophisticated over 20s. Dine, Wine, Dance.' Its marketing was aggressive, with Mondays being 10p night, the price for any drink from the bar.

A new decade is usually a signal for change, especially in terms of popular culture where new generations are eager to put the past behind them and create their own unique identity. But the early Baby Boomer generation which danced through the 1960s will always argue that there was never a better time to be young.

CHAPTER 4: DANCING DOWN THE PUB

1960s Hotels, Pubs and Social Clubs

Besides the Ballrooms that were frequented by Derby's dancers, several hotels, public houses, and social clubs had the facilities to present public and private dance events.

Local, amateur rhythm groups, beat groups, blues and jazz bands were springing up all over Britain from the early 60s and Derby had its fair share. Pubs with function rooms and a decent dance floor soon got in on the

The Blue Peter, Alvaston

The memories of Di Dinsdale, Allestree

I was there!

One of my most memorable nights dancing in Derby wasn't at one of the established ballrooms or clubs, but at the Chaddesden Park Hotel which was really a pub. The Steam Packet with Rod Stewart, Long John Baldry and Julie Driscoll were performing. I was star struck and managed to get their autographs. Straight after that night I styled my hair differently, not like Rods, but like Julie Driscoll's.

My first job was working as a hairdresser at Marden and Mayfield which was owned by Stan Fowkes, one of the owners of Clouds. He put a small salon into the club where I would work some evenings and helped collecting glasses. But one night, after I had taken the empties to the bar, the hinged bar top fell and broke all the glasses. I didn't get the sack, but Mr Fowkes deducted the cost from my full-time hairdressing salary. When Jim Milton, the manager, found out he made sure that I always got in free at Clouds after that.

Di after seeing Julie Driscoll

Fashion was very important to me in those days and I often made my own miniskirts. I would be down at the open market early on a Friday morning to buy fabric. The prices were so cheap, especially as half a yard would do for my miniskirts. I also managed to get unusual, but fashionable, shoe samples in styles and colours that you wouldn't have seen on the high street, and only costing around 2/6 a pair (25p).

Another fond memory from those days is that my father always made sure I had four penny coins in my hand-bag before I went out. He would say "If you ever miss the bus or run out of money just phone me from a call box and I'll come and fetch you." How did we manage without mobiles?

act and, most weekends, would present 'live' music for dancing, and later on, DJs.

The evenings would sometimes feature a visit from the Kershaws seafood vendor and perhaps members of the Salvation Army selling *The War Cry* or *The Young Soldier* magazines.

MINSTREL BAR
DISCOTHEQUE
at the
TIGER BAR
CORN MARKET
DERBY

Charrington well-known beers

ADMISSION FREE
[STRICTLY LIMITED]

Cloak Room

RIGHT OF ADMISSION RESERVED

The Crown Hotel, Allenton

Derby's larger hotels would hold traditional dinner/dances, especially over the Christmas period and some establishments were brave enough to present Nationally known chart acts.

Dancing down the pub

Some of the venues that regularly presented music for dancing during the 1960s

Hotels and Pubs

Angler's Arms
Nottingham Road, Spondon

Bell Hotel
Sadler Gate

Blue Boy
Wiltshire Road, Chaddesden

Blue Peter
Alvaston

Blue Pool
Sunny Hill

Chaddesden Park Hotel
Nottingham Road, Chaddesden

Coppice Hotel
Chain Lane, Littleover

Coronation Hotel
Baker Street, Alvaston

Corporation Hotel
Cattle Market

Crown Hotel
Osmaston Road, Allenton

Derbyshire Yeomanry
Kingsway, Mackworth

Drill Hall
Newland Street

Friary Hotel
Friargate

Grandstand Hotel
The Racecourse

Midland Hotel
Railway Terrace

Moon Hotel
Spondon

Nags Head
Derby Road, Mickleover

Old Bell Hotel
Sadler Gate

Osmaston Park Hotel
Osmaston Park Road

Penguin
Chaddesden

Tiger Bar
Lock-up Yard

Wheel Hotel
Friargate

Windmill Inn
Breadsall Hill Top

Social Clubs

Alvaston British Legion

Borrowash Ex-Servicemen's Club

Crown Club
Nottingham Road, Spondon

Chellaston British Legion
Derby Road, Chellaston

Pastures Hospital Social Club
Mickleover

Railway Institute
Siddals Road

Rolls-Royce Welfare Club
Moor Lane

The Author

Roger Smith has music running through his veins. At the 'birth' of British pop in the early 60s he was playing bass guitar in Derby semi-pro groups The Rapids and Godfreys Grit'n'Soul Band. By the middle of the 'Swinging Sixties' he temporarily hung up his Fender bass and spent his spare-time helping to establish Derby's Soul scene with Discovery Discotheque, Clouds and Shotgun Discotheque.

Roger worked at The Derbyshire Advertiser and The Derby Evening Telegraph for many years and in 1975 joined Derby County Football Club, then Football League Champions, as Advertising and Sponsorship Executive. He formed Smith East Associates in 1977, with Trevor East, and the business became one of the region's leading advertising agencies. He has lived in Derby all his life and is still working as a marketing consultant, but still finds time to thump out 60s rock'n'roll, soul and pop with Godfreys Grit'n'Soul Band, just as he did more than 50 years ago.

The Gaumont pop concerts encapsulated an era of great music, great musicians and it formed the bedrock of Derby's growing music scene. It was Roger Smith's life blood and he was a major part of it all in those exciting, heady times.

We Danced in Derby is a chronicle of the 1960s, when Derby's music got toes tapping and bodies gliding over the polished floors of dance halls, clubs, Discos and even some pubs. Let the words and photos transport you to the dancing, music and even clothes of an era that lives on in our memories. Time travel with a beat that gets the heart racing and smiles broadening.

By Richard Cox, a member of the renowned Derby Evening Telegraph 'Saturday Page' crew from 1970 to 1977.

Thanks

The author would like to thank the following for their help with this book:

David Foster: Design collaboration and artwork

All the 'I Was There' contributors

Derby Telegraph Photo Library

Derby Local Studies Library

Thanks also for the help advice and encouragement received from:
Paul Blackmore, Ross Coe, Geoff Cook, Trevor East, Patrick Flood,
Judy Handsley, Haydn Harris, Winifred, Anthony and Gill Holland, Lis
Kolkman, Len Lancaster, Denis Lynch, Glen Lynch, Dave Milton, Lynne
Milton, Graham (Norwax) Norman, Martin (Macca) Payne, Anton Rippon,
Chris Sharratt, Doug Smith, Ron Taylor, Kip Wilks, and finally, to my
dear wife Maria for putting up with another two years of my periodic,
virtual absence.

Another title by the author

WHEN THE STARS CAME TO TOWN
chronicles over forty shows that visited
Derby's largest cinema between 1959 and
1966 and shares the memories of people
who were there. It also presents a fascinating,
previously unpublished, collection of
photographs of some of these stars taken
while of they were in the city.

For more information, please visit
www.thetapmarketing.com/publishing
or contact
enquiries@thetap-publishing.com

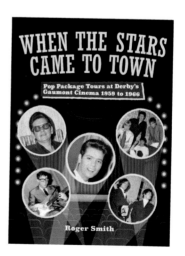